The Money Instinct

Why Your Brain Sabotages Your Money (and the Money Scripts That Explain It)

PART OF THE MONEY INSTINCT LIBRARY

Jordan Ellis

First edition, 2026

Published by Jordan Ellis

Contents

Foreword

I didn't set out to write a book about psychology. I set out to figure out why smart, careful people — including me — keep making the same money mistakes on repeat, for years, despite knowing better in the moment right after.

That's the specific stake I have in this. Not a dramatic story, no theatrical bottom. Something quieter and more common: a stretch of years where I could recite sound financial advice back word for word and still watch myself act against it an hour later, sometimes the same day. Reading a budgeting book didn't fix it. Reading five didn't either. What eventually helped wasn't more advice. It was understanding that the part of me making those decisions wasn't listening to advice in the first place — it was running on older software, reacting to triggers most personal-finance books never even mention.

That gap is the whole reason this book exists. Most money advice assumes a rational actor sitting quietly at a desk, weighing options, choosing correctly once given the facts. That actor is a fiction. The real decision-maker is faster, older, and was built for a world with no credit cards, no countdown timers, no infinite scroll — and it is still running the show more often than any of us would like to admit.

I wrote this book for the version of you that already knows the right answer and does the other thing anyway. You're not weak. The fight was never fair to begin with, and nobody told you that going in.

This is a field guide, not a confession and not a cure — a map of a machine every one of us is carrying around, written by someone who spent a long time getting outrun by his own instincts before learning to build around them instead of arguing with them. If any of the patterns in the pages ahead land closer to home than expected, you're not broken. You're just finally looking at the machine instead of blaming yourself for what it does.

That's the whole reason I sat down to write this.

— Jordan Ellis

Introduction — The Argument in Your Head

There is a small argument that happens in your head every time money is involved.

One voice wants the thing. The coffee, the upgrade, the "treat yourself," the sell button, the not-looking-right-now. It's fast, certain, and it feels like you. The other voice already knows how this ends. It's quieter. It usually shows up about a day too late, doing the math you didn't want to do.

You've met both voices. You know the second one is usually right. And yet the first one keeps winning — not because you're weak, or bad with money, or undisciplined. It keeps winning because it was built to win. It's older than your rational mind by a few hundred million years, and it is very, very good at its job.

This book is not about budgets. There are a thousand books about budgets, and if a spreadsheet was going to fix this, it already would have. You don't have a math problem. You have a **pattern** problem — a set of predictable, wired-in moves your brain makes with money, the same way it makes you flinch at a loud sound. You can't delete them. But once you can *see* them, you can get in front of them. That half-second of seeing is the whole game.

Consider, for a moment, what these two voices actually sound like when they take turns. The fast voice doesn't announce itself as reckless — it never says "let's be impulsive." It says something closer to "you deserve this," or "you've earned it," or "everyone else already has one," or "this won't matter in the long run anyway." It borrows the language of self-respect and proportion to make its case, which is exactly why it's so hard to catch in the moment: it doesn't feel like giving in. It feels like a reasonable person making a reasonable call. The slower voice, when it finally arrives, rarely sounds triumphant either. It usually sounds tired, a little embarrassed, doing arithmetic it wishes it had done twenty minutes earlier. Neither voice is a villain in this story. They're both you, running on different clocks, optimized for different jobs — and the entire premise of this book is that the fight between them isn't fair, not because one side is weak, but because the fast voice gets there first, every single time, unless something in the structure of the decision buys the slow voice enough time to show up before it's too late to matter.

What follows are the eight patterns that quietly cost people the most — not in dramatic, one-time disasters, but in the slow leak of a hundred small decisions that never felt like decisions at all. Overspending that feels like living. Saving that feels like loss. Avoiding the numbers because looking feels worse than not knowing.

Each chapter does four things. It shows you the pattern in a moment you'll recognize. It tells you honestly what's actually happening underneath — the real mechanism, no mysticism. It names what the pattern costs you. And then it gives you one specific override: a small, doable move that gets your slower, smarter voice into the room *before* the decision instead of after.

You don't need to master all eight. Most people find that one or two of these are the ones running their life, and fixing just those changes the whole picture.

One more thing before we start, because it will save you some frustration later: you will recognize yourself in more than one of these chapters, possibly in most of them, and that's not a sign you're unusually broken. It's a sign you're a normal human being with a normally-wired brain operating in an environment built to trigger exactly this wiring as often and as reliably as possible. The point of naming eleven separate patterns isn't to hand you eleven separate problems. It's to give you eleven separate, specific handles on what has probably always felt, from the inside, like one vague, undifferentiated feeling of being bad with money. Vague feelings are hard to fix. Specific, named mechanisms, each with its own specific override, are not.

A note on what this book is not: it is not financial advice. It won't tell you what to buy, sell, or invest in — that's not the problem, and it's not my place. This is about the mind that sits behind every one of those choices. Get that right, and the rest gets a great deal easier.

Let's go meet the first pattern. You already know it well.

Chapter 1 — The Machine You Didn't Install

Why willpower was never going to be enough

Somewhere along the way, you were handed a piece of machinery you never asked for, never chose, and can't return. It came fully assembled, running software written for a world that no longer exists, and it has been quietly steering a portion of your financial life ever since — not because you're careless, and not because you lack discipline, but because the machine was built for a different job than the one it's currently doing.

This chapter is about that machine. Not any single pattern yet — those come next, eleven of them, each its own chapter. This one is about the thing underneath all eleven: the single reason none of them can be fixed the way most advice assumes they can be fixed, and the reason this book is built the way it is instead.

Picture two people standing in front of the same ATM receipt. One glances at the balance, feels a small flicker of unease, and moves on with their day, mentally filing it as "something to look at eventually." The other feels the same flicker and, within the hour, has bought a pair of shoes they weren't planning to buy that morning. Same machine, same species, same balance, wildly different outputs — and neither of them chose their response the way they'd choose an outfit. The response arrived pre-loaded, faster than the conscious mind could weigh in, built from a combination of old wiring and a lifetime of specific reinforcement that neither of them designed on purpose. This is what it looks like when the machine runs unexamined: not a single dramatic failure, but a thousand small forks in the road, each one resolved before you knew there was a decision to make.

The world the machine was built for

Your brain's core wiring around risk, reward, status, and scarcity was substantially shaped over a period of human history spanning hundreds of thousands of years — a period defined by conditions almost nothing like the ones you make financial decisions in today. Resources were scarce and unpredictable. A bad season could be lethal. Standing within a small group determined access to food, safety, and mates. Rewards, when they came, came slowly and were rarely certain. A mind built to navigate that world developed a specific set of priorities: notice threats fast, weigh losses heavily, care intensely about relative status, prefer certain-now over uncertain-later, and conserve resources aggressively whenever things felt tight.

None of that was irrational. It was, in fact, extremely well-calibrated to the actual conditions your ancestors faced, for as long as those conditions held. A mind that ignored status was a mind whose owner didn't get chosen for alliances that mattered. A mind that didn't panic at sudden loss was a mind whose owner didn't survive the sudden losses that were, historically, often genuine emergencies. Every pattern in this book, examined on its own terms, is a reasonable response to the world it was built for. The machine isn't broken. It's just running in the wrong environment.

The mismatch

Here's what changed, and how fast it changed, measured against how long the machine had to adapt to the previous conditions: modern financial life — credit, instant digital purchases, decades-long compounding, abstract numbers on a screen standing in for real resources, a media environment engineered specifically to exploit every one of these ancient priorities — is, on the timescale that shaped your underlying wiring, essentially brand new. It arrived far too recently, and far too fast, for the machine underneath it to have had any chance to update.

So you're left with a genuine mismatch, and it's worth being precise about what kind of mismatch it is, because getting this right changes everything about how you respond to it. This isn't a mismatch between a good machine and a bad one. It's a mismatch between a well-built machine and a world it was never calibrated for. The instinct that made a hunter-gatherer's mind light up at the sight of a rare, high-status object is the same instinct that lights up at a designer jacket today — except today, that instinct can be triggered dozens of times a day, satisfied with one tap, and financed on credit, none of which existed in the environment the instinct evolved to handle. The instinct that made loss feel more urgent than an equivalent gain is the same instinct that pulls you to sell at the bottom of a market — except today, the "loss" is a number on a screen that may recover in months, not a genuine, permanent depletion of resources the way most losses were for most of human history.

There's a version of the mismatch worth tracing through the scarcity instinct specifically, because it shows up in a place that has nothing to do with actual resource shortage: the "limited time offer," the "only 3 left in stock," the countdown timer on a webpage. The ancestral machinery that made scarcity genuinely dangerous — a truly limited food source, a truly limited window of opportunity — reads these signals with the same urgency it would apply to a real, once-in-a-season chance that might not come again. It has no mechanism for distinguishing a manufactured, infinitely-repeatable "limited time offer" running on a loop from a genuinely rare, non-repeating opportunity, because that distinction simply didn't need to exist in the environment the instinct evolved in. Scarcity, for almost all of human history, was expensive to fake — creating a false shortage took real effort and real resources. Today it costs nothing to display a countdown timer that resets the moment you close the tab, which means the signal the instinct is built to trust has become nearly free to manufacture, and nobody told the instinct.

Trace a single decision all the way through and the mismatch stops being abstract. A notification arrives — a price drop, a "your cart is waiting," a headline about a falling market. The ancient machinery reads it as new, salient information demanding a response, exactly as it would have read a sudden rustle in tall grass: orient, assess, act. It has no mechanism for recognizing that this particular signal was engineered, by a team of people whose job is specifically to produce that orienting response as often and as reliably as possible, in exchange for your attention or your money. The rustle in the grass, ten thousand years ago, fired rarely and meant something. The notification fires constantly and usually means nothing except that someone, somewhere, has gotten very good at making it feel like it does.

Here's a version of the mismatch that has nothing to do with shopping or markets, which is useful precisely because it strips away the more obvious examples and shows the underlying shape more clearly. Your ancient status instinct evolved to track your position within a tight, physically bounded group — the people you'd actually see, compete with, rely on. It had no way to distinguish "the forty people in my actual life" from "the several hundred loosely-connected acquaintances and strangers my phone shows me a curated glimpse of every day," because that second category simply didn't exist for the overwhelming majority of the time period the instinct was calibrated against. So the instinct does what it has always done: it runs the comparison, faithfully, against whatever population gets placed in front of it — except the population in front of it now is larger, more selectively curated toward its best moments, and less representative of ordinary life than any group a human status instinct ever had to measure itself against before. The instinct isn't malfunctioning. It's functioning exactly as designed, against an input the design never anticipated.

The environment is getting more extreme, not less

Here's the part that makes this more urgent than it might otherwise seem: the gap between the machine and its environment isn't stable. It's widening, and it's widening on purpose. Every mechanism in this book — the dopamine loop, the status comparison, the scarcity tunnel, the loss-driven panic — is now the direct target of enormous, sophisticated, continuously optimized effort, because triggering these mechanisms reliably is worth an extraordinary amount of money to whoever manages to do it. A retailer in 1955 had a fixed storefront, a print catalog, and limited ways to catch your attention. A retailer today has a live, constantly-tested feed calibrated, often algorithmically, to find exactly the presentation that triggers your specific version of the dopamine loop most reliably — and it gets to run that experiment on you millions of times, refining itself a little further every time it learns something.

There's a specific dynamic worth naming about how this optimization actually happens, because it isn't a single company sitting down once and designing a perfect trap. It's closer to an evolutionary process running at business speed: thousands of retailers and platforms run constant, small experiments — this button color against that one, this notification wording against that one, this layout against that one — and the versions that trigger the strongest response survive, get scaled up, and become the new default, while the versions that don't quietly disappear. Nobody needs to fully understand the dopamine loop or loss aversion by name for this process to find and exploit them; the market-level selection pressure finds what works empirically, the same blind, iterative way evolution itself found what worked over a much longer timescale. This is part of why the systems trying to trigger these patterns keep getting better even without any single person deliberately engineering the improvement — the improvement emerges from the aggregate of millions of small tests, most of which you'll never know happened, run against you and people just like you, continuously, in the background of ordinary browsing.

This means the honest starting assumption for the rest of this book isn't "these patterns exist and I should be aware of them." It's "these patterns exist, they are being actively and expertly triggered by systems built for exactly that purpose, and the sophistication of those systems is only increasing." That's not a reason for despair — it's the reason structural overrides matter more than willpower ever could. Willpower is a fixed, limited resource facing an opponent that gets more sophisticated every year. A structural override, once built, doesn't care how sophisticated the opponent gets, because it doesn't rely on you winning a fair fight in the moment. It relies on the fight never happening at all.

The machine learns your specific triggers, not just the general ones

Here's a layer that makes this even more personal than "humans are wired for scarcity in general": the machine doesn't just run the species-wide defaults. It gets fine-tuned, over your specific lifetime, by whatever happened to be reinforced along the way — a process the psychologist Albert Bandura spent much of his career mapping under the concept of self-efficacy, the learned belief, built from direct experience and observed example, about what you are and aren't capable of controlling. If your early experience of money was chaotic — a household where spending felt erratic, where scarcity struck without warning, where nothing you did seemed to change the outcome — your machine doesn't just inherit the general human scarcity instinct. It inherits a specific, personal calibration that says *control isn't really available to you here*, and that calibration will quietly shape which of the eleven patterns in this book hits you hardest, years before you ever open a bank statement as an adult.

This is worth sitting with, because it explains something that pure evolutionary psychology can't: why two siblings, raised in the same house, can grow into wildly different relationships with money. The general machine is shared. The specific tuning isn't. One sibling's machine got calibrated toward hoarding and hypervigilance; the other's got calibrated toward avoidance and denial — different overrides on the same base hardware, installed by different specific experiences of watching money behave unpredictably around them. Neither calibration is a character flaw. Both are the machine doing exactly what machines do: learning from whatever data it was given, without the ability to ask whether the data was representative of the world it would actually have to operate in as an adult.

The practical upshot is that this book's eleven patterns won't hit you all with equal force, and the reason isn't random. It's your specific tuning, laid on top of the species-wide wiring, and part of what the "read all eleven, notice which ones land" instruction later in this chapter is actually asking you to do is locate your own calibration — not just find the generic human bugs, but find the specific version installed in you.

Why information alone doesn't fix this

Here is the single most important thing this book asks you to actually absorb, because almost everything that follows depends on it: knowing about a pattern is not the same as being free of it. You can read the dopamine-loop chapter, understand precisely why anticipation outpaces having, nod along with the neuroscience — and still feel the pull the next time a shopping app puts a countdown timer on a deal. That isn't a failure of comprehension. It's proof the mechanism is doing exactly what it was built to do, and what it was built to do doesn't reroute itself just because the conscious, reasoning part of your mind now understands the mechanism intellectually.

This is why traditional financial advice so often doesn't stick, even when it's correct. "Spend less than you earn." True, and useless on its own, the same way "don't feel afraid" is true and useless to someone standing at the edge of a genuinely frightening height. The instruction is aimed at the wrong layer of the system. It's trying to reason with a part of the mind that doesn't process reasons — it processes triggers, rewards, threats, and comparisons, running mostly beneath the level where information alone can reach it.

There's a name in psychology for part of what's happening when information alone fails to change behavior, and it comes from Steven Hayes's work on acceptance and commitment: the distinction between the content of a thought and a person's relationship to that thought. Knowing a shopping app's countdown timer is manufactured urgency is content — a fact, held intellectually. Feeling the pull of that timer anyway, despite knowing, is about your relationship to the urge in the moment it arrives, and that relationship doesn't automatically update just because the content of your beliefs did. Hayes's broader clinical work suggests that trying to argue yourself out of a felt urge, purely through better facts, is a strategy with a poor track record precisely because urges aren't fact-checking operations to begin with — they're older, faster, and largely indifferent to what the reasoning mind has concluded. This is a clinical, well-tested version of the exact claim this chapter is making about money specifically: you don't defeat an urge by out-arguing it. You defeat it by changing what happens structurally in the moment it arrives, which is the whole design philosophy behind every override in the chapters ahead.

What actually works: override, not overhaul

If information doesn't fix the machine, and you can't uninstall it, what's left? This is the actual thesis of the book, stated plainly, so you can hold it as a frame for everything that follows: you don't fix an old machine by arguing with it. You fix it by building a specific, structural override for each specific behavior it produces — a small design change that gets the slower, more accurate part of your mind into the decision *before* the old machine's momentum carries you past the point where reasoning still has a say.

There's a useful way to test whether a proposed fix is a genuine structural override or just willpower wearing a disguise: ask whether it would still work on the worst day you can imagine having — exhausted, stressed, distracted, emotionally raw. "I'll try to spend less" fails this test instantly; a tired, raw version of you is precisely the version least equipped to try harder at anything. "The shopping apps are deleted from my phone, so buying something requires re-downloading an app first" passes the test, because it doesn't ask anything of tired-you at all. It was already built by rested-you, in advance, and it keeps working regardless of what state you're in when the moment arrives. Run every override in this book through that same test as you build it: does this still work on the worst day, or does it quietly require you to be your best self to function? If it requires your best self, it isn't finished yet.

This is closer to engineering than to self-improvement, and that distinction matters more than it might seem to at first. Self-improvement asks you to become a different, more disciplined person — a project with no clear finish line, vulnerable to a bad day, a tired week, a moment of low willpower undoing months of effort. Engineering asks something much smaller and much more durable: identify the specific mechanism, build a specific structure that interrupts it at the right moment, and let the structure do the work a tired, distracted, ordinary Tuesday version of you could never be relied on to do through willpower alone. A twenty-four-hour rule doesn't require you to feel strong. An automated transfer doesn't care whether you're motivated today. That's the whole design philosophy behind every override in this book: build something that works even on the days you don't.

Consider what this looks like in practice, before you've even reached the chapters that name each specific pattern. Two people decide, on the same January morning, that they're going to stop overspending on takeout. The first relies on willpower: a firm internal decision, renewed every evening around 6pm when the tired, hungry, decision-fatigued version of them stands in the kitchen weighing a fifteen-minute cooking task against a three-minute app order. Most evenings, tired-them wins, because willpower is a resource that happens to be lowest exactly when the temptation is highest — the two are correlated, not independent, which is precisely why relying on willpower to intervene at the point of temptation is such a structurally bad bet. The second person builds an override instead: groceries delivered on a fixed schedule, a short list of ten-minute meals kept visible on the counter, the food-delivery apps deleted from the phone so ordering requires a deliberate, multi-step detour instead of a single tap. Neither person is more disciplined than the other. But the second person's good decision was made once, on a rested Sunday afternoon, and then simply kept happening on their behalf every tired weeknight after — which is the entire difference between hoping the machine behaves and building something that works regardless of how it behaves.

This isn't unique to money

If this framework — override the structure, not the person — sounds familiar, it's because it's the same insight underneath most durable behavior change, in domains that have nothing to do with money. The person who successfully builds a consistent exercise habit rarely does it through raw willpower alone; they change the environment so the desired behavior becomes the default one, laying out the clothes the night before, choosing a gym on the route already driven. The person who quits a habit successfully usually isn't relying on saying no more forcefully in the moment of temptation; they remove the cigarettes from the house, delete the app, make the unwanted behavior structurally harder to access than the wanted one. None of this is really about money-specific psychology. It's about a much older, more general truth: environment beats intention, almost every time, for almost everyone, because intention is a finite resource that has to be renewed daily, and environment just sits there, quietly doing its job, whether you're feeling strong that day or not.

There's a specific reason money deserves its own book rather than a chapter inside a general behavior-change guide, beyond the adversarial-pressure argument already made: money is unusual in how many of the other patterns it touches at once. A habit like smoking engages roughly one or two of the mechanisms in this book — the dopamine loop, mostly, and perhaps some social performance around it. Money engages nearly all eleven, often simultaneously, in a single decision. Buying a car can trigger the dopamine loop in the anticipation of the purchase, the status instinct in the model chosen, the anchor in the sticker price, the endowment effect the moment you drive it off the lot, and present bias in whether you finance it in a way that discounts a future you'd rather not think about yet. Few other domains of life stack this many mechanisms into single, ordinary decisions as routinely as money does, which is part of why a fix aimed at any one pattern in isolation so often feels incomplete — the other patterns are usually still running in the background of the exact same decision.

Money is simply one of the highest-stakes arenas where this general truth plays out, because unlike most other domains, money decisions are engineered against, constantly, by systems with a direct financial incentive in your failure to override them. That's the specific reason this book exists as a money book rather than a general behavior-change book — not because the underlying mechanism is different, but because the adversarial pressure is unusually intense and unusually well-funded here, which makes structural overrides not just useful but close to necessary.

How to read what follows

Each of the next eleven chapters follows the same shape, deliberately, because the shape itself is part of the point: first, a moment you'll recognize — the machine caught in the act, doing exactly what it always does. Then, the actual mechanism underneath it, named plainly, sourced honestly, without mysticism or exaggeration. Then, what the pattern actually costs you, made concrete enough to feel rather than just know. And finally, the override — not a vague call to try harder, but a specific, structural move designed to get your slower, more accurate judgment into the room at the exact moment the machine's momentum would otherwise carry the decision on its own.

There's one more framing worth holding as you read, because it will keep you from a specific trap this book's own structure could otherwise lead you into: don't read the coming chapters as a diagnostic checklist looking for what's wrong with you. Read them as a field guide to a machine that every reader of this book, without exception, is running — some patterns louder than others, none entirely absent. The person who reads all eleven chapters and finds nothing that lands as personally true hasn't been paying close enough attention. That's not because they're unusually well-adjusted — it's because these patterns are, as established, close to universal features of the wiring, not personal failings that only some people happen to carry. The question was never whether the machine is running in you. It's only ever been which parts of it are running loudest, and what you're going to build in front of them now that you can see them clearly.

You won't need all eleven with equal urgency. Almost everyone finds that one or two of these patterns are doing the overwhelming majority of the damage in their specific life, while the others are present but minor. Read all eleven once, honestly, and notice which ones land like a description of a stranger and which ones land like a description of you. Build the overrides for the ones that land. That's the whole method — not eleven simultaneous life overhauls, but a handful of specific, structural corrections aimed precisely at the machine you actually have, running in the world you actually live in.

One last practical note before you move to Chapter 2: as you read each of the following eleven chapters, resist the urge to immediately implement every override on a first pass. The chapters are sequenced deliberately, but you're free to read them out of order, skip ahead to whichever title catches you hardest, and come back for the rest later. What matters more than reading order is what you do after you finish any single chapter that lands: stop, build the one override it describes, let it run quietly for a few weeks before adding another. Eleven overrides built in a single burst of motivation rarely survive contact with an ordinary week; two or three built one at a time, each one already working on autopilot before the next gets added, tend to still be running a year later. This book rewards patience more than it rewards enthusiasm, and that's by design — the whole premise, again, is that structure beats willpower, including the willpower it would take to overhaul eleven habits simultaneously.

The machine was never the enemy here. It kept every ancestor you have alive long enough to have you. It just never got the update — and this book is that update, delivered one override at a time.

Chapter 2 — The Dopamine Loop

Why your brain is wired to overspend

You're not going to buy anything. You're just looking.

You open the app to check one thing — a price, an order, a notification — and twenty minutes later there's a small pile in the cart. None of it is unreasonable. Each item has a little story: you *needed* a new one, it was *on sale*, you've *earned* it, it was *practically free* at that price. You check out. There's a warm little click of completion. For about an hour, maybe a day, things feel slightly better.

Then the box arrives, and the strange part happens: opening it is quieter than buying it was. The thing is fine. You're glad to have it. But the feeling you were actually chasing already came and went — and it came *before* the package, not after.

That timing is the entire secret, so hold onto it: **the good feeling arrived at the moment of anticipation, not the moment of arrival.**

There's a version of this loop that shows up specifically around payday, and it's worth naming because it can feel like the opposite of impulsiveness — it can feel responsible. The direct deposit lands, and within the same day, sometimes the same hour, a chunk of it is already gone: a purchase that had been "planned" for weeks, sitting in a cart, waiting only for funds to clear. The planning makes it feel deliberate rather than impulsive, and in one narrow sense it is — you didn't buy on a whim. But watch the timing closely and the same mechanism is running underneath: the anticipation had been building for weeks, spiking hardest right as the money became available, and the purchase itself, once made, produced the same brief lift followed by the same quiet fade the impulse version produces. Planning ahead doesn't switch off the loop. It just gives the loop a longer runway and a better disguise.

You've felt the other version of this too, the one that doesn't even end in a purchase. The wishlist you keep adding to but rarely buy from. The saved items, the "maybe later" folder, the browser tabs left open on things you have no real intention of getting today. If the point were really the having, an unpurchased wishlist should feel like pure frustration — want without resolution, over and over. Mostly it doesn't. There's a specific, low-grade pleasure in the browsing and the adding itself, separate from whether anything ever gets bought. That's the anticipation system running on its own, decoupled entirely from acquisition, proving the point better than any purchase could: the machinery was never really about the getting.

There's a version of this that plays out over months instead of minutes, and it's easier to miss because no single moment feels like a purchase decision at all. Think about the last time you renovated a room, or planned a trip, or built out a hobby from scratch. The actual event — the finished kitchen, the week away, the fully-kitted-out setup — occupied a handful of days. The *planning* of it occupied weeks, sometimes months: browsing options, comparing, imagining how each choice would feel, building the thing in your head long before you built it in your life. People who are honest about it will often tell you the planning was the best part — not despite being separate from the actual having, but *because* it was separate from it. The anticipation phase ran uninterrupted, for weeks, unbothered by the comparatively brief and often disappointing reality of the thing itself finally arriving. If you've ever felt a small letdown after a long-anticipated purchase or trip finally happened — a sense of "that's it?" that you couldn't quite explain — this is why. You'd already spent the good part.

What's actually happening

Most people think of the buy-button rush as the brain rewarding you for getting the thing. It isn't. Your reward system runs mostly on a chemical called dopamine, and dopamine is not the chemistry of *pleasure* — it's the chemistry of *anticipation*. It doesn't spike when you get the reward. It spikes when your brain predicts one is coming.

This is one of the most reliable findings in modern neuroscience, and it's a little unsettling once you see it clearly: the wanting and the having run on different systems. Wanting is loud, forward-leaning, and chemical. Having is quieter and fades fast. Your brain will happily generate an enormous amount of wanting for something that delivers a small, brief amount of having. It is not trying to make you happy. It is trying to keep you *moving toward things*, because for most of human history, moving toward things — food, resources, status — is what kept your ancestors alive.

There's a useful piece of vocabulary from researcher Kent Berridge's neuroscience work that clarifies exactly what's splitting apart here: Berridge and collaborators distinguish between "wanting" (the dopamine-driven motivational pull toward a reward) and "liking" (the actual, separate pleasure of experiencing it), and one of the more striking findings from that research is that these two systems can be pulled apart from each other, sometimes dramatically. Wanting can run at full intensity while liking barely registers at all — which is a precise, clinical description of exactly what the empty feeling after a purchase actually is. It isn't that the thing failed to deliver pleasure because it was a bad purchase. It's that the wanting system, which was doing nearly all of the emotional work leading up to the purchase, simply has very little left to hand off to the liking system once the transaction completes, because the two were never as connected as they feel like they should be.

A shopping app is a machine built, deliberately, to pull that lever as many times per minute as possible. The scroll, the deals, the "only 3 left," the one-tap checkout — every piece of it exists to maximize *anticipation*, because anticipation is the part that feels good, and the part that feels good is the part that makes you come back. You are not shopping. You are being administered small, precise doses of a chemical you make yourself.

There's a specific, almost paradoxical version of this loop worth naming: the purchase you make specifically to end the wanting, which instead extends it. Buy the thing you've been anticipating for weeks, and instead of the anticipation quietly switching off, it often just relocates — to the next thing, the accessory that would complete it, the upgraded version you now notice exists. This isn't a coincidence or bad luck. It's the anticipation system doing exactly what it's built to do: find the next target the instant the current one is neutralized, because a system built to keep you moving toward things doesn't have an "off" setting once it's warmed up. It has a "redirect" setting. This is part of why a single purchase so rarely satisfies the way it promised to — not because the purchase was wrong, but because satisfaction was never really the mechanism's actual goal.

There's a specific version of the loop worth naming that operates in reverse of ordinary shopping: the compulsive comparison-shopping spiral, where the anticipated reward isn't a product but the *feeling of having found the best possible deal.* Someone caught in this version can spend hours across multiple tabs and apps chasing a marginally better price on something they were already going to buy, and the actual money saved, once you count the value of the hours spent chasing it, is frequently negative. The dopamine here isn't attached to the product at all — it's attached to the hunt, the anticipation of the win over the price itself, which is why the spiral rarely stops the moment a genuinely good price is found. It stops, if it stops, only when something external interrupts it, because the hunt was never really trying to end.

None of this means the wanting is fake or that you're broken for feeling it. The instinct is doing exactly what it evolved to do. The problem is only that it evolved in a world where wanting something and *getting it instantly, on credit, at 11pm, in two taps* were never the same event. Now they are. The gap the instinct used to rely on — the days or weeks between the urge and the ability to act on it — is gone. And that gap was doing more work than anyone realized.

There's a layer of design specificity worth naming, because it explains why some categories of shopping pull harder than others: the loop is strongest wherever the reward is both frequent and *varied* — new items, new combinations, new arrangements — rather than a single static product you either want or don't. This is part of why certain categories, the ones with the deepest, most constantly refreshed catalogs, produce more of this pattern than categories with a small, fixed set of options. A narrow product line runs out of novelty quickly, and the anticipation system, once it's seen everything on offer, has nothing left to spike about. An enormous, constantly rotating catalog never runs out, which means the loop, in that category, never has a natural stopping point built into the inventory itself. You have to supply the stopping point yourself, because the store isn't going to run out of new things to dangle.

There's a second layer to the engineering that makes this loop especially hard to walk away from: unpredictability. A reward that arrives every single time you take an action is powerful, but a reward that arrives *unpredictably* — sometimes yes, sometimes no, on a schedule you can't quite map — is more powerful still, and more resistant to fading. This is the same basic mechanism behind why a slot machine is more compelling than a vending machine, even though a vending machine always delivers and a slot machine almost never does. Certainty lets the anticipation system relax once it learns the pattern. Unpredictability keeps it fully engaged indefinitely, because it can never fully learn the pattern. A shopping feed that shows you an amazing find one time in twenty, on no fixed schedule, is running exactly this mechanism. It's not an accident that so much of modern shopping has been redesigned, deliberately, to feel more like a feed you scroll than a catalog you browse.

There's a related concept worth naming here, because it explains why the loop feels so specifically compulsive rather than just mildly pleasant: psychologist Robert Zajonc's research on the "mere exposure effect" found that repeated exposure to a stimulus, on its own, with no other change, increases how favorably people feel toward it. Scroll past the same category of product enough times and your baseline warmth toward it rises, quietly, through nothing more than repetition — which means a shopping feed doesn't even need to show you anything genuinely new to strengthen the pull. Simply showing you variations on the same theme, over and over, does real psychological work, priming you to feel more favorably disposed toward a purchase you hadn't consciously been building a case for at all. The feed isn't just exploiting anticipation. It's also manufacturing familiarity, and familiarity, to a mind that didn't evolve around infinite scrolling, reads as a kind of trustworthiness it hasn't earned.

What it costs you

There's a workplace variant worth naming too, because it's easy to miss when you're only looking at consumer shopping: the "productivity purchase," the tool, app subscription, or system bought specifically to solve a problem you're anticipating rather than one you currently have. The planner that will finally organize you, the course that will finally teach you the skill, the software that will finally fix the workflow — each one riding the exact same anticipation spike as a shopping-app purchase, dressed up in the more respectable language of self-improvement and investment in yourself. The graveyard of unused productivity tools sitting quietly in most people's digital lives is the receipt for this version of the loop: purchases made almost entirely for the anticipated feeling of finally being organized, rarely followed by the sustained use that feeling implied would happen next.

Here is why this one matters more than it looks. Nobody goes broke from a single impulse buy. This pattern doesn't hurt you in dramatic amounts — it hurts you in *frequency*. It's the leak, not the flood.

Run the honest number sometime: the small, anticipation-driven purchases, the ones that never felt like real decisions, added up across a year. For most people it's not a rounding error. It's a vacation. It's the emergency fund they keep meaning to build. It's the exact gap between "I don't know where my money goes" and knowing. The money didn't go anywhere dramatic. It went, five and fifteen and forty dollars at a time, toward a feeling that had already faded by the time the box arrived.

And there's a second cost, quieter than the money: every time the loop runs and the having disappoints, you learn, a little, to distrust yourself around money. That erosion is its own tax.

The override

You cannot out-willpower a system older than your species. Willpower is the slow voice trying to win a race it enters late. So you don't fight the wanting — you **reintroduce the gap** the modern world deleted.

Watch for the loop disguised as productivity. Because the loop wears a more respectable costume in the form of "productivity purchases," apply the same 24-hour gap to tools, courses, and subscriptions bought in anticipation of becoming more organized or capable, not just to obviously discretionary shopping. If you already own an unused tool that once promised to solve the same problem, that's a strong signal the anticipated fix is really this chapter's mechanism wearing a work-related disguise.

The 24-hour gap. For any non-essential purchase above a number you choose — say, whatever feels like "a bit much" for you — you're allowed to want it as much as you like. You just can't have it today. Put it in the cart, close the app, and set it down for one day. That's the whole rule.

Here's why it works, and it isn't about discipline. The wanting is a *spike* — it's designed to be intense and brief. Twenty-four hours is longer than the spike can hold. When you come back the next day, you're not fighting the urge, because the urge is simply gone; you're now making the decision with your slower voice, the one that was always going to arrive eventually. You're not denying yourself the thing. You're just letting the *right* part of your brain be the one that decides. About half the time, you'll find you don't want it anymore — which tells you it was never the thing you wanted. It was the spike.

One more move, for the purchases that don't clear a 24-hour buffer — the quick, in-person, small ones. Before you buy, **name the feeling, not the item.** Not "I want this coffee/gadget/shirt," but "I'm bored," "I'm celebrating," "I had a hard day," "I want to feel like the kind of person who has this." Naming the feeling does something almost unfairly simple: it hands the moment to your slower voice, because *the slow voice is the only one that can name things.* The instinct doesn't narrate. The moment you put words to what you're actually reaching for, you've already stepped half an inch outside the loop — and half an inch is enough to choose.

Interrupt the comparison-shopping spiral specifically. If you recognize the hunt-for-the-best-price version of this loop in yourself, give it its own dedicated rule: set a firm time limit — fifteen minutes, say — for comparing options on any single purchase, and commit in advance to buying the best option found within that window rather than continuing to search. The spiral thrives on having no natural stopping point; a pre-committed limit supplies one artificially, which is often all it takes, since the spiral was never really optimizing for the best price to begin with.

Starve the unpredictability, on purpose. Because the loop is strongest when the reward feels unpredictable, one of the most effective structural moves is to remove yourself from the environments engineered to deliver it — unsubscribe from the retailer emails, turn off the app notifications, delete the shopping apps from your phone's home screen so reaching them requires a deliberate search instead of a habitual tap. This isn't about willpower in the moment; it's about reducing how often the slot-machine mechanism gets a chance to fire at all. A lever you don't walk past doesn't get pulled nearly as often, no matter how strong the pull would have been if you had.

Redirect the anticipation on purpose, toward something that compounds. Because the good feeling really is the wanting and not the having, you don't have to eliminate anticipation to break the loop — you can point it somewhere else entirely. Open a specific savings goal with a name and a visible number, and let yourself check it, watch it grow, imagine what it becomes, with the same idle curiosity you'd otherwise spend browsing a shopping app. The anticipation system doesn't care whether the thing it's anticipating is a package or a growing number; it just wants something to track and something to look forward to. Give it a target that gets better the more you feed it, instead of one that quietly resets the moment the box arrives.

The rule to remember: *The good feeling is the wanting, not the having. Let the wanting pass, and you rarely lose anything but the wanting.*

Chapter 3 — The Creep

Why earning more leaves you with exactly the same

Think back to the last real raise you got. Not a cost-of-living bump — a genuine step up. A new job, a promotion, a jump in what you bring home.

Remember the feeling. There was a specific fantasy attached to it, and the fantasy was almost never about the money itself. It was about what the money meant: *now I can breathe. Now the tight months are over. Now I'll finally save the way I keep meaning to.* You could feel the slack it was going to create — the distance between what you earned and what you needed, opening up like a window.

Now answer honestly: how long did that window stay open?

For most people, the answer is a few months. Maybe less. The raise arrived, the breathing room appeared exactly as promised — and then, without any single decision you could point to, it closed. Not through anything reckless. There was no blowout, no yacht, no moment of madness. Just a slightly nicer apartment because the old one was genuinely getting cramped.

A better car, because the old one was becoming a liability. Groceries that cost a bit more because you stopped checking prices, and why should you, you'd earned that. The gym, the subscriptions, the takeout on the nights you were too tired to cook — each one reasonable, each one *deserved*, each one arriving so quietly that none of them felt like the thing that ate the raise.

But something ate the raise. Here you are, earning meaningfully more than the version of you who once dreamed about this exact income — and you have the same amount left at the end of the month. Sometimes less. The window opened, and then the room grew to fill it, and now you're standing in a bigger room with the same amount of air.

This is the second pattern, and it is the quietest thief in the whole book. It doesn't take from you in a moment you'd notice. It takes from you in the shape of a life that keeps expanding to swallow whatever you feed it.

There's a specific version of this that plays out around major life transitions — a wedding, a first home, a new baby — where the creep arrives all at once instead of gradually, because an entire category of spending gets reset in a single season rather than eroding slowly over years. Couples planning a wedding routinely watch their own budget climb, line by line, as each individual upgrade gets justified against the last one rather than against any outside standard: the venue justifies the catering tier, the catering tier justifies the florals, and by the end, a number that would have seemed absurd at the start of the process feels not just reasonable but almost restrained, purely because of the sequence of internal comparisons that led there. Nobody along the way made an obviously bad decision. Each choice was reasonable relative to the choice just before it. The creep, compressed into months instead of years, is still the same mechanism — anchoring to the most recent decision instead of to any fixed outside reference.

It isn't only raises. Watch how quickly a single splurge becomes the new floor for an entire category of spending. The one nice dinner out becomes, within a few months, the baseline expectation for what "going out" costs — not because you decided that consciously, but because the cheaper version now registers as a downgrade rather than a return to normal. The upgraded flight becomes the minimum acceptable way to travel. None of these individual shifts feel like decisions. Each one just feels like *this is what things cost now*, and that quiet, invisible resetting of "normal" is the exact same mechanism running at a smaller scale, one category at a time, well before an actual raise is ever involved.

Watch it play out in a different arena entirely and the shape becomes unmistakable: two friends both get modest windfalls the same year — an inheritance, say, or a bonus large enough to matter. One puts it toward a down payment and keeps living exactly as before; within a year, the money is invisible, folded into a mortgage payment that simply replaced a rent payment, no felt change in day-to-day life at all. The other uses it to upgrade almost everything at once — car, apartment, wardrobe, the whole visible texture of daily life — and within that same year, none of it feels like an upgrade anymore either. It just feels like Tuesday. Both windfalls were identical in size. Both produced, after twelve months, an identical felt sense of "this is just my life now." The only real difference is that one of them left a lasting asset behind, and the other left a permanently higher cost of standing still.

What's actually happening

There's a mechanism underneath this, and once you see it you'll recognize it everywhere — not just in money, but in almost everything you've ever wanted.

Your brain does not measure how good things are on an absolute scale. It measures *change*. It's built to notice the difference between what's happening now and what was happening a moment ago, and then — this is the crucial part — to go quiet once the new level becomes normal. Psychologists have a name for this: adaptation. The older, blunter nickname is the *hedonic treadmill*, and the image is exact. You get the better thing, you feel the lift, and then you adapt to the better thing until it becomes your new baseline — the new floor from which the next lift will be measured. You're running, and the ground moves under you, and you end up in the same place.

The first taste of anything good is vivid. The tenth is wallpaper. The first week in the nicer apartment, you notice the extra light, the quiet, the space — it feels like proof that your life is working. By month three you don't see any of it. It's just where you live. The pleasure didn't last because it was never designed to last. Its entire job was to mark the *change*, and once the change is complete, the feeling has done its work and switches off.

There's a specific finding from well-being research worth naming here, because it puts a number on something this chapter has so far only described qualitatively: studies tracking life satisfaction after major positive life events — a large financial windfall being one of the more heavily studied examples — have repeatedly found that reported happiness rises sharply at the time of the event and then returns, within a period that's often surprisingly short, to something close to the person's pre-event baseline. This doesn't mean the windfall did nothing; the person is still, materially, better off. It means the *felt* sense of "how good is my life right now" is far more tethered to the trajectory of recent change than to the absolute level of resources available, which is precisely the treadmill mechanism this chapter is describing, now with actual measurement behind it rather than just intuition.

Understand what this means and you'll stop blaming yourself for it: the fade is not a personal failing or a sign you're ungrateful. It is the correct functioning of a system that evolved to keep you moving. A creature that stayed permanently satisfied by its last success would have had no reason to seek the next meal, the next improvement, the next bit of safety. Your ancestors were the ones who felt the lift and then, crucially, felt it fade — because the fade is what sent them looking again. You are descended from a very long line of the chronically unsatisfied, and that dissatisfaction kept them alive.

The trouble is the same trouble that runs through this entire book. The instinct was built for a world where "the next improvement" meant a better tool or a safer shelter — things that were hard to get and stayed got. It was not built for a world where the next improvement is one tap away, endlessly, at every price point, marketed to you by people who understand the treadmill better than you do and have arranged their entire business around it. In that world, an appetite that was supposed to keep you alive becomes an appetite that quietly consumes every gain you ever make.

And here is the specific trap with money, the reason lifestyle creep is more dangerous than plain overspending: it disguises itself as progress. Buying something you can't afford feels like a mistake, and at least a mistake announces itself. But upgrading your life to match a raise you actually earned doesn't feel like a mistake at all. It feels like *arriving*. It feels like the whole point. Nobody feels guilty about the nicer apartment — they feel like they've finally made it. The creep hides inside the most legitimate feeling you have: the sense that you've earned a better life. That's what makes it so hard to catch. It isn't dressed as weakness. It's dressed as success.

There's a related idea in psychology sometimes called adaptation-level theory, which describes how a person's judgment of "normal" isn't fixed — it's recalibrated continuously based on recent experience, so that the same objective circumstance can feel like a windfall to one person and a disappointment to another, purely depending on what each of them had adapted to just before. This is why two people earning the identical income can have wildly different felt experiences of "enough" — not because one is more grateful or more disciplined, but because their adaptation-level baselines were set by different recent histories, and each of them is unconsciously measuring the present against their own personal, constantly-shifting version of normal rather than against any objective standard.

There's a further layer here from social psychologist Leon Festinger's broader work on comparison — not just comparison to other people, which shows up in its own right in the next chapter, but comparison across *time*, against your own recent past. The reference point your mind uses to judge "is this good" isn't fixed to any absolute standard; it's continuously reset to whatever you most recently experienced, which means the very act of experiencing an upgrade destroys the reference point that made the upgrade feel like one. You are, in a very literal sense, chasing a target that moves specifically *because* you're chasing it — every gain becomes the new zero line the instant it's achieved, which is what makes lifestyle creep so different from ordinary overspending. Ordinary overspending is a decision you can catch. This is a recalibration your mind performs automatically, with or without your permission, every single time your circumstances improve.

What it costs you

Let me make this concrete, because in the abstract it sounds almost harmless — so what if my spending rose with my income? Isn't that the reward for working hard?

Here's the cost. Every time your lifestyle rises to match a raise, you don't just spend the raise once. You reset your *baseline* — the amount your life now requires to run. And that new baseline is permanent in a way the raise is not. The raise can vanish: a layoff, an illness, a bad year, a downturn that has nothing to do with you. But the lifestyle you built on top of it doesn't shrink nearly as easily, because your brain has already adapted to it. That nicer apartment isn't a treat anymore; it's just where you live, and moving out of it now feels like *going backward* — like a demotion, a failure — even though it was a luxury eighteen months ago. You've been quietly turned into a person who needs more to feel normal.

So the real cost isn't the money that got absorbed, though that's real too. The real cost is that lifestyle creep steals the one thing a raise was supposed to buy you: *options*. Freedom, honestly measured, is not how much you earn. It's the gap between what you earn and what you need — because that gap is the space where all your choices live. The gap is what lets you leave a job that's hurting you, weather an emergency without panic, say no, take the risk, walk away. Every time you let your needs rise to meet your income, you spend that gap. You can be earning three times what you earned a decade ago and be *less* free, more trapped, more terrified of losing it all — because you've built a life that requires every dollar of it just to stand still.

There's a specific version of this cost worth naming around career choices, where lifestyle creep quietly forecloses options that would otherwise be genuinely available. A person whose expenses have risen to consume their full income finds themselves unable to take a lower-paying job that would offer better hours, more meaningful work, or a healthier environment — not because the lower-paying job wouldn't be worth it in every way that matters, but because the lifestyle built on top of the higher income has become load-bearing, and removing that load feels, and in the near term genuinely is, destabilizing. The creep doesn't just steal a general, abstract sense of freedom. It can steal a specific, concrete opportunity that was sitting right there, fully available, to a version of you with a smaller baseline.

That's the trade almost no one realizes they're making: they trade their freedom for a slightly nicer version of a life they'll stop noticing in ninety days. They pay in the only currency that actually mattered, for a lift that was never going to last, to impress a sense of "having arrived" that moves one step further away every single time they reach it.

Run your own number, gently. Take what you earn now and what you earned five years ago. The difference is large — larger, probably, than the version of you back then would have believed. Now ask where it went. Not the dramatic answer. The honest one: it went into a baseline that quietly rose to meet it, dollar for dollar, until the breathing room you were promised had been fully converted into a bigger room to breathe the same amount of air in.

The overrides

You can't switch off adaptation. It's not a bug you can patch; it's the operating system. But you can get in front of it, because the creep depends on one specific weakness: it only works when the upgrades happen *automatically and invisibly*, decided by default rather than on purpose. Make the decision conscious and you break the spell. Here are three ways.

Pre-commit the raise before it arrives. The creep does its damage in the gap between getting more and deciding what to do with it — because in that gap, "just live a little better" is the path of least resistance, and the money gets absorbed before you ever chose anything. So close the gap. Decide, *in advance*, what happens to the next raise, before you ever feel it in your account. The rule that works for most people is simple: split it. When more money arrives, a fixed share of the increase — half is a strong number — goes straight into the gap (saved, invested, toward the goal) automatically, on the day the raise starts, before it ever touches your spending. You still get to enjoy the other half; this isn't about denial. But you enjoy it *on purpose*, from a smaller pool, instead of letting the whole raise dissolve invisibly into a baseline you never agreed to. The money you never see, you never adapt to. That's the whole trick: adaptation can't get its hooks into money that was gone before you got used to it.

Protect the career options the creep would otherwise foreclose. Before a lifestyle upgrade becomes permanent, ask specifically: would this upgrade, once absorbed, rule out a job change, a career pivot, or a lower-stress option I might genuinely want in the next few years? This isn't a reason to never upgrade anything — it's a way of pricing the upgrade honestly, in terms of the specific future flexibility it costs, rather than only in terms of its monthly dollar figure.

Run the same-life audit. Once a year, look hard at the upgrades you've absorbed and ask a brutal question of each one: *if this disappeared tomorrow, would I actually be less happy — or have I just adapted to it?* You'll find the honest answer is often the second one. The subscription you forgot you had. The "nicer" version of something whose nicer-ness you stopped registering months ago. The bigger space you use a third of. These aren't things you enjoy; they're things you've merely gotten used to, which is a completely different thing — the treadmill made them your floor without ever giving you lasting pleasure in return. Cancel or downsize the ones that are pure baseline with no live joy in them, and here's the part that surprises people: you won't feel the loss for long, because adaptation runs in both directions. You adapt *down* to a smaller life almost as fast as you adapted up to a bigger one. The dread of going backward is far worse than the reality, which fades in a few weeks, just like everything else.

Watch for compressed creep around major transitions. Because lifestyle creep can happen in weeks instead of years during a wedding, a move, a new baby, or any season with many sequential upgrade decisions in a row, treat these periods with extra scrutiny. Before each individual choice, briefly step outside the sequence and compare it against a fixed outside reference — what would this specific item cost if you were pricing it fresh, with no prior decisions in the sequence to anchor against — rather than only against the choice immediately before it. This interrupts the internal-comparison chain that makes compressed creep so easy to miss while it's happening.

Anchor to an old baseline on purpose. The creep works by quietly moving your reference point up, so that each new level of spending feels normal and the next upgrade feels reasonable. You can fight it by deliberately holding an old reference point in place. Pick a version of your life from a few years ago — a leaner one you remember being genuinely fine in — and keep it as your mental baseline, the thing "normal" is measured against, even as your income climbs. Not out of self-punishment; out of clarity. When "normal" stays anchored low and your income rises above it, the difference doesn't vanish into a bigger life — it stays visible, as the gap, as options, as the growing distance between what you have and what you need. The people who get genuinely wealthy almost all do a version of this: they let their income rise and refuse to let their baseline chase it. That refusal *is* the wealth. It was never the earning.

Track the creep across major life transitions specifically. Around a wedding, a move, a new baby, or any season with a rapid sequence of upgrade decisions, keep a running total of the increase in fixed monthly cost the season is producing, updated after each individual choice rather than only tallied at the end.

Seeing the compounding total in real time counters the internal-comparison chain that makes each individual choice feel small and reasonable in isolation.

Name the finish line before you start running toward it. Part of what makes the creep so persistent is that "enough" is rarely defined — without a concrete target, every new level of income just becomes the new midpoint, with more always feeling like the correct next direction. Pick a specific, honest number: an income, a lifestyle, a savings rate that would genuinely feel like enough, not aspirational, not impressive to anyone else. Write it down. A moving target guarantees the treadmill keeps running. A fixed one gives you somewhere to actually arrive.

The rule to remember: *A raise you spend is gone in ninety days; a raise you keep is freedom that lasts. Your life will always expand to swallow your income — unless you decide, on purpose and in advance, that it won't.*

Chapter 4 — The Audience That Isn't There

Why you buy things to impress people who aren't watching

You buy the jacket. Not because you need a jacket — you own jackets, functioning ones, ones that keep the rain off exactly as well as this one will. You buy it because of a very specific, very brief flash of imagination: someone you know seeing you in it. A particular person, maybe, or a particular kind of room. You picture the version of yourself wearing it and you picture, just as vividly, someone else *noticing*.

Here's the part that's almost too uncomfortable to say out loud: you can probably name the person. Not always a real, specific human — sometimes it's a composite, an old classmate merged with a coworker merged with nobody in particular — but if you're honest, most status purchases have an audience attached. A silhouette in your mind who is watching, and reacting, and revising their opinion of you upward.

Now the harder question. When was the last time that person actually saw the jacket, registered it, and said anything about it at all? Not "did they compliment it" — did they even *notice*? For the overwhelming majority of the things bought for this exact reason, the honest answer is: never. The audience you were performing for wasn't just unimpressed. They weren't in the room. Some of them, if you trace it back far enough, aren't even in your life anymore — you're still buying for the approval of people from a decade ago who have no idea you exist.

You didn't buy the jacket for you. You bought it for a witness who was never going to show up.

There's a version of this pattern that operates entirely within a peer group rather than toward a general, imagined public, and it can be even more expensive because the audience, this time, is at least partly real. A friend group where one person buys a bigger house, or a nicer car, or takes a more extravagant trip can produce a kind of quiet, unspoken arms race among the rest of the group — not because anyone announces a competition, but because each person's sense of "appropriate for someone at my level" gets recalibrated by what they've just seen a peer do. The audience here isn't imaginary in the way the composite stranger from earlier is; these are real people, genuinely watching, at least some of the time. But the actual financial damage still vastly outweighs the actual social stakes involved — losing a friend's good opinion over a smaller car is a far smaller cost, examined honestly, than the years of financial strain taken on to prevent a loss of standing most of that friend group barely tracks in the first place.

It shows up in smaller, stranger ways too, once you know to look. The choice of restaurant, weighted more by how the reservation will sound mentioned in passing than by whether you actually want the food. The vacation photographed more than it's experienced, chosen partly for how well it will read as a set of images to an audience that will glance at them for two seconds each, forget them within the hour, and never think of the trip again. None of this is unique to any one platform or generation — it's simply that the instinct now has more surfaces than ever to perform on, and less of a real, present audience checking whether the performance was worth the cost.

Watch it operate in a setting with genuinely no audience at all, and the pattern gets even stranger. Someone redoes a guest room that guests almost never use, choosing a higher-end finish "in case someone sees it" — a someone who, if you actually count the visits, amounts to a handful of people across several years, most of whom wouldn't register the difference between the finish chosen and the cheaper one sitting right beside it on the showroom floor. The room isn't being decorated for the people who'll use it. It's being decorated for an audience that exists almost entirely in the decorator's own head, rehearsing a moment of being seen that, statistically, will happen perhaps twice a year, for people who came to see the host, not the finish on the guest room floor.

What's actually happening

This isn't vanity, and it isn't a character flaw, even though it can feel like one in the cold light of the credit card statement. It's a specific, well-documented piece of social wiring, and once you see the mechanism, the jacket makes a strange kind of sense.

Human beings are, more than almost any other trait, a status species. For most of our history, standing within the group wasn't a nice-to-have — it was survival infrastructure. Higher status meant better access to food, safety, mates, allies who'd back you when it mattered. A brain that didn't care where it stood relative to everyone else was a brain attached to a body that didn't make it very far. So evolution built you an extremely sensitive, always-on instrument for measuring your position — and, critically, for noticing anything that might *raise* it.

The psychologist Leon Festinger gave this its formal name in the 1950s: social comparison theory — the idea that people determine their own worth largely by measuring themselves against others, especially others they see as similar to them. You're not comparing yourself to billionaires or monks; you're comparing yourself to the people one rung over, one rung under, close enough that the comparison feels live. And there's an older, blunter cousin of the same idea from the economist Thorstein Veblen, writing well over a century ago: *conspicuous consumption* — spending not to use a thing, but to display it, because the display itself is the point. Veblen watched people in his own era buy things specifically so the buying could be seen, and correctly guessed that this wasn't a passing fashion. It was structural.

Put those two together and you get the actual mechanism behind the jacket. Your status-measuring instinct is running constantly, comparing you to a rotating cast of "similar others" — and it treats a *visible upgrade* as one of the fastest ways to move the needle. Not because the jacket makes you warmer or more capable. Because the jacket is *legible* — it can be seen, categorized, and priced at a glance by anyone who knows what to look for, which makes it an unusually efficient tool for the one thing the instinct actually wants: to be read, instantly, as having gone up a level.

Here's where the modern mismatch comes in, and it's a particularly cruel one. For most of human history, "the group" was small — a village, a clan, forty or fifty people you'd actually interact with, whose opinions of you had real, ongoing consequences for your life. The instinct evolved to care about *that* audience, an audience that was small, present, and paying attention because they had to — your standing among them genuinely mattered to their own survival calculations too.

Now the instinct is still running the same program, but the "audience" it's calculating for has become almost entirely imaginary. It's built from fragments: a highlight reel of people you follow but rarely speak to, a memory of someone who made you feel small once, a generalized sense of "people" that has no actual faces attached to it anymore. The instinct doesn't know the difference. It still performs the calculation with the same urgency it would use for the forty people whose opinion once decided whether you ate that winter — except now it's running that calculation for an audience of nobody, made of everybody, watching from nowhere in particular.

There's a specific irony worth sitting with here: the more curated and public a modern audience becomes, the less it actually functions like the small, real audience the instinct evolved for. A feed of loosely-connected acquaintances offers none of what the ancestral group actually provided — no real reciprocity, no real safety net, no real stake in each other's outcomes — while still fully activating the ancient status-tracking machinery built for exactly that kind of high-stakes, reciprocal group. You end up paying the full emotional and financial cost of an ancient social contract while receiving almost none of its actual benefits, because the modern audience was never a real group in the first place. It's a crowd, and a crowd, unlike a tribe, owes you nothing.

There's a related concept from sociologist Erving Goffman worth naming directly, because it captures something the Festinger and Veblen frameworks don't quite reach on their own: Goffman described everyday social life as a kind of ongoing performance, in which people manage a "front stage" self — curated, presented, aware of being watched — distinct from the more unguarded "backstage" self that exists when no audience is assumed to be present. Status spending is front-stage spending almost by definition: it exists specifically for the version of you that's on display, which means an enormous amount of it is, structurally, spending on a self you don't actually get to inhabit most of your life. The irony Goffman's framework surfaces is that the backstage self — the one buying nothing, performing for no one, simply living — is the self doing almost all of the actual living, while the front-stage self absorbs a disproportionate share of the budget for a much smaller share of the time.

What it costs you

The money is the obvious cost, and it's real — status purchases carry a specific premium precisely because visibility is the product, not the underlying thing, and visible things are reliably marked up over their functionally identical, less legible equivalents. But the deeper cost is the one that doesn't show up on a receipt.

Every dollar spent performing for an audience that isn't there is a dollar that can't be spent on anything the audience-that-isn't-there will never notice regardless — which, when you actually sit with it, is almost everything that makes a life good. Your emergency fund is invisible to onlookers. Your retirement account is invisible. The fact that you could handle a surprise expense without panic is completely invisible, right up until the moment it isn't, and by then it's not a status signal, it's just relief. None of the things that make you genuinely secure are legible from across a room — and so the instinct, which is only built to notice what's visible, systematically under-funds every one of them in favor of things that can be seen.

There's a career-specific version of this cost worth naming, because status spending doesn't only show up in visible consumer goods — it shows up in career choices made for how they'll sound rather than for what they'll actually provide. The prestigious job title chosen over the better-fitting role, the impressive-sounding employer chosen over the one that would have paid more or offered a healthier environment, both driven by the same audience-performance mechanism, just operating on a decade-long timescale instead of a single purchase. The cost here compounds especially hard, because unlike a jacket, a career choice made for its audience-facing value can quietly steer years of a working life in a direction chosen for a witness who, once again, mostly wasn't watching closely enough to justify the trade.

There's a second cost too, quieter and stranger: the performance rarely satisfies even the imagined audience. Because the instinct is calibrated to a moving target — you compare yourself to people slightly ahead of you, and the moment you catch up, your reference point simply resets to the next tier — the jacket doesn't end the comparison. It just moves the finish line. You can run this treadmill for a lifetime, spending real money to impress an audience that was never watching, in order to feel briefly ahead of a line that immediately redraws itself one step further out. That's the actual trap: not that the audience doesn't exist, but that even a *real* audience wouldn't have ended the chase, because the chase was never about them. It was about a status instrument that doesn't know how to switch off.

Run the number gently, the way we did with the raise. Not the price of any one purchase — the pattern across a year. The things bought specifically to be seen, categorized, priced-at-a-glance by people who, if you're honest, mostly weren't looking. For a lot of people that number is startling not because any single decision was foolish, but because none of them individually felt like "showing off" — each one felt like a reasonable little upgrade. It's only in the aggregate that the shape becomes visible: a meaningful fraction of a life's spending, aimed at an audience that was composed, this whole time, of people who weren't there.

The overrides

You cannot switch off status-sensitivity. It is not a flaw to be willed away; it's part of the same wiring that makes you capable of belonging to a group at all, and a person with none of it would be a person with none of the instincts that make community possible. What you can do is stop letting an *imagined* audience make decisions a *real* life has to pay for.

The "who's this for?" test. Before any purchase where visibility is doing real work in the decision — the upgrade, the version that photographs well, the thing that will be seen — ask the question directly and answer it specifically. Not "would people like this," which the instinct will always answer yes to. *Who, specifically, is this for? Name them.* Most of the time you'll find one of two things happens. Either you genuinely can't name anyone — the audience dissolves the moment you look directly at it, which tells you everything — or you *can* name someone, and naming them makes the whole transaction feel smaller and stranger than it did a moment ago, because it's hard to keep performing once the performance has a specific, ordinary face attached to it instead of a vague, flattering blur. Either way, naming the audience breaks the spell that vagueness was protecting.

Audit career decisions for audience-driven weighting, not just purchases. Before accepting a role, a title, or a career move, separate out explicitly how much of its appeal comes from what it does for your actual working life versus how it will sound described to other people. If the second category is doing most of the emotional lifting, treat that as a warning sign worth sitting with rather than a settled reason to proceed — the audience for a career choice made mostly for its sound is, per this chapter's whole argument, unlikely to be paying nearly as much attention as the decision assumes.

The three-day social fast, before any large discretionary purchase. Status purchases are triggered disproportionately by recent exposure — a feed scrolled, a gathering attended, a comparison freshly made. The instinct is loudest right after it's been fed a fresh reference point. So for anything above a threshold that feels significant to you, build in three days with no social media, no browsing the kind of content that shows you what other people have, before you finalize the purchase. This isn't about willpower in the moment of buying — by the time you're at checkout, the instinct has usually already won. It's about not feeding it the comparison in the first place. Most people find that a want which felt urgent on day one has gone quiet by day three, because the specific trigger — someone else's visible upgrade — has faded, and what's left is a much smaller, much more honest question: do I actually want this, or did I want to have *had* it in front of someone?

Separate real peer feedback from imagined general audience. When a status purchase is triggered by an actual peer's actual purchase, rather than a vague general audience, treat it as its own distinct case rather than folding it into the same response as the composite-stranger version. Ask directly: is the discomfort here about a real relationship dynamic worth addressing honestly with that specific person, or is it the same imagined-audience mechanism wearing a real person's face because they happened to be the one who triggered it? Most of the time it's the latter — the friend's new car didn't actually change how they see you, only how you, briefly, imagined they might.

Build a real scoreboard and put it somewhere you'll see it. The instinct needs *something* to compare against — that part of it isn't optional, and trying to eliminate comparison entirely just leaves a vacuum the old, status-driven comparison will refill. So give it a better scoreboard on purpose. Pick the numbers that are actually invisible to onlookers but genuinely determine how your life goes — months of expenses saved, debt paid down, the gap between what you earn and what you need — and track them somewhere you'll actually see, the way you'd once have tracked a visible status marker. Over time, the instinct that used to light up at a compliment on a jacket can be retrained to light up at a number moving in the right direction, because it was never attached to jackets specifically — it just needs *a* signal that things are improving, and you get to decide which signal that is.

The rule to remember: *Almost no one is watching, and the ones who are won't remember. Spend for the life only you will ever fully see.*

Chapter 5 — The Anchor

Why a crossed-out price can change what something is actually worth to you

A jacket hangs on the rack with two numbers on the tag. The first one has a line through it. The second one, underneath, is what you'll actually pay.

Look at how your own mind moves through that tag, in order. First it reads the crossed-out number — and for one unguarded second, that number becomes the jacket's *real* price, the one the universe assigned it. Then it reads the second number, the one you'll actually pay, and something in you relaxes, because that number is *less than* the real price. You didn't just find a jacket. You found a deal. The jacket could be worth exactly what you're paying and not a cent more — plenty of jackets are — but for that one unguarded second, the crossed-out number did its work, and its work was to make the second number feel like a gift instead of a price.

Nobody set that first number honestly, and somewhere you probably know that. Prices get marked up specifically to be marked down. The two numbers were never really two facts about the jacket's worth — the first one was written to make the second one land. And it worked. Not because you're gullible. Because your mind isn't built to judge a price on its own. It's built to judge a price *against whatever number it saw first.*

It works the same way in reverse, and this version is subtler because there's no crossed-out number in sight. A subscription service offers three tiers — a modest one, a middle one, and an expensive one nobody's really meant to choose. The expensive tier isn't there to sell itself. It's there to anchor the middle one, making a genuinely mediocre deal feel like the sensible, moderate choice by comparison. You end up congratulating yourself on your restraint, having avoided the "too much" option, while paying more than you would have if the middle tier had simply been presented on its own, with nothing expensive sitting beside it to make it look reasonable.

It shows up in a completely different register during salary negotiations, and this version is worth sitting with because so many people walk directly into it without noticing. A recruiter asks, early in the process, what salary range you're currently expecting — a routine, almost throwaway question. Whatever number you give in that moment becomes the anchor for the entire negotiation that follows, regardless of what the role is actually worth or what the company had budgeted for it. Name a number lower than the role's real value, even slightly, and you've just handed the other side an anchor that will pull every subsequent offer downward, no matter how skilled a negotiator you turn out to be for the rest of the conversation. Name a number with real confidence, closer to the top of a reasonable range, and the entire negotiation reorganizes itself around a higher gravity well instead. The strange part is how little the actual back-and-forth matters once the anchor is set — most of the real outcome was decided in that first, almost casual exchange, long before either side started "negotiating" in the way people usually picture it.

What's actually happening

This is one of the best-documented quirks of the human mind, and it has a name: anchoring. Once your brain is given a number — any number, even one it has every reason to distrust — that number becomes a kind of gravity well. Every judgment you make after it gets pulled toward it, even when you consciously know the number is arbitrary or engineered.

The finding traces back to research by the psychologists Daniel Kahneman and Amos Tversky, who ran a version of this experiment that has since become famous: they had people spin a wheel that was secretly rigged to land on either a low number or a high number, then asked an entirely unrelated question — something like, what percentage of a certain group of countries belong to a particular organization? The wheel had nothing to do with the answer. And yet the group that spun the high number guessed significantly higher than the group that spun the low number. A number with zero logical connection to the question still dragged the answer toward it. That's the anchor at work, in its purest, most absurd form — and if a random spinning wheel can do that to your estimate, a carefully chosen price tag, engineered by someone whose job is to move you, does it far more effectively.

There's a related effect worth naming that compounds anchoring rather than replacing it: the framing of a number, independent of the number's actual size, changes how it's received. A price described as "just three dollars a day" and a price described as "over a thousand dollars a year" can be the identical figure, restated, and yet land completely differently, because your mind doesn't automatically do the multiplication or division required to compare the two framings on equal footing — it takes whichever number is handed to it and anchors around that specific framing. Subscription pricing, in particular, is very often deliberately presented in its smallest, most anchor-favorable unit for exactly this reason: three dollars a day sounds trivial in a way that the same commitment, restated honestly as an annual total, plainly is not.

Why would a mind work this way? Because judging value in a vacuum is genuinely hard, and your brain, like most efficient systems, prefers *comparison* to *calculation from scratch.* Is this jacket worth what I'm paying? That question, asked honestly, requires you to weigh the material, the craftsmanship, how often you'll wear it, what else that money could do — real work. Is this jacket worth less than that other number I just saw? That question is easy. It's not even really math. It's just a direction: up or down from the anchor. Your mind takes the easy question because it's faster, and most of the time, fast is fine. The problem is that the easy question only works if the anchor itself is honest — and the anchor is very often not honest. It's placed.

There's a version of anchoring that operates through comparison to *other people's* purchases rather than through a marked-up price tag, and it can be just as powerful while feeling completely different in character. Hear that a colleague paid a certain amount for a service, or a friend mentions what they spent on a similar item, and that number quietly becomes your anchor for the entire category going forward, regardless of whether it reflects the actual market or simply one specific, possibly unrepresentative transaction. You end up pricing your own decision, without realizing it, against a single overheard data point rather than against a genuine, honest survey of what the thing is actually worth — the same gravitational pull as the crossed-out tag, just arriving through conversation instead of a price sticker.

Once you start looking for anchors, you find them everywhere, because they're not a retail trick specifically — they're a general-purpose lever on human judgment, and anyone selling anything eventually discovers it. The overpriced item at the top of a menu that nobody's expected to order, there to make the second-priciest item look reasonable by comparison. The "originally $1,200" sticker on a mattress that never sold for $1,200 a day in its life. The real estate agent who shows you one wildly overpriced house first, so the second house — the one they actually wanted you to buy — lands as a relief. None of these need you to believe the anchor is real. They only need your mind to register it, because registering is enough to move the comparison.

There's a deepened version of the mechanism worth understanding, because it explains why anchoring survives even when you *know* the number is fake. Kahneman later described this as part of a broader distinction between two modes of thought: a fast, automatic, intuitive mode, and a slower, deliberate, effortful one. Anchoring is, fundamentally, a fast-mode operation — it happens before the slow mode even gets a chance to weigh in, which is why simply *knowing* a price was inflated for the markdown doesn't stop the anchor from doing its work. Your slow, reasoning mind can label the anchor as manipulative and still watch, almost as a bystander, as your fast mind's sense of "what's reasonable" gets dragged toward it anyway. This is different from most cognitive biases people imagine they can simply "know their way out of." Anchoring doesn't operate at the level knowing operates on. It operates one layer beneath it, in the same fast system that decides, before you've consciously thought about it, whether a shadow in your peripheral vision is worth turning your head for.

What it costs you

The direct cost is the easiest to see and probably the smallest part of it: you pay more, on average, for things whose price you judged relative to an anchor than for things you priced blind. That adds up, quietly, across a life of purchases — but it's not actually the expensive part.

The expensive part is what anchoring does to your sense of what things are *actually* worth, which compounds far past any single purchase. Every time you accept an anchor without noticing it, you're training your own internal sense of value to be led rather than to lead. You stop asking "what is this worth to me" and start asking "is this a good deal relative to what I was just shown" — and those are two entirely different questions with two entirely different owners. The first one is answered by you. The second one is answered by whoever set the anchor. Do that enough times, across enough purchases, and your sense of value quietly becomes outsourced — not to a person, but to whatever number happens to be sitting nearby when you make a decision.

There's a specific, painful version of this that shows up around big-ticket purchases, where the anchor isn't a crossed-out price but a number a salesperson gives you early and confidently: the "starting at" figure, the sticker price on a car built to be negotiated down from, the opening ask in a negotiation. Real estate provides one of the clearest large-scale examples: a home listed deliberately above what the seller actually expects to get functions as an anchor for every buyer who views it, and even buyers who negotiate hard and feel triumphant about the discount they secured are still, in absolute terms, measuring their win against a number the seller chose specifically to be negotiated down from. The entire theater of the negotiation — the back-and-forth, the counteroffers, the sense of hard-fought progress — can produce a satisfying feeling of victory while the final number still sits comfortably inside the range the anchor was designed to produce in the first place. Once that number lands, everything that follows gets measured against it, including the final number you settle on — a number that can still be, in absolute terms, far more than the thing is worth to you, and yet feel like a win purely because it's less than the first number you heard. You can walk away from a negotiation feeling triumphant and still have paid more than you would have priced the thing on your own, with no anchor in the room at all. The feeling of winning and the fact of overpaying are not mutually exclusive. That's the whole danger of the mechanism — it doesn't just change what you pay, it changes how you *feel* about what you paid, and the feeling is what stops you from noticing.

The overrides

You can't switch off the anchoring reflex — no one can; it's not a personality trait, it's how comparison-based judgment works in every human mind that's ever been tested for it. What you can do is control which numbers get to act as your anchor, instead of accepting whichever one happens to be placed in front of you first.

Prepare your opening number before any salary or negotiation conversation. Because the first figure exchanged in a negotiation anchors the entire conversation that follows, research a defensible, confidence-supporting number in advance for any negotiation you know is coming, and be the one who names a number first wherever the context allows it. Letting the other side anchor first, even in something as routine-feeling as a recruiter's opening question, hands away leverage before the substantive conversation has even begun.

Price it blind before you see their number. Before you look at the sticker, the crossed-out figure, the "starting at," ask yourself, on your own, with no number in the room yet: what would I be willing to pay for this, based only on what it does for my life? Write that number down, or at least hold it firmly in your head, before you expose yourself to theirs. This sounds almost too simple to matter, but it works because of exactly the mechanism that makes anchoring dangerous in the first place —

whichever number arrives *first* becomes the gravity well. If your own honest number gets there first, their number has to work against your anchor instead of the other way around. You've flipped who's doing the anchoring.

Always convert small-unit framing back to the full commitment. Whenever a price is presented in its smallest possible unit — daily, per-use, "less than a coffee" — deliberately do the multiplication yourself and evaluate the full annual or total figure instead, before deciding. This isn't the same move as the per-use conversion below; it runs in the opposite direction, undoing a framing trick rather than applying a clarifying one, and both are useful because sellers can anchor you with either direction depending on which one favors them.

Convert the price into something anchor-proof: the per-use cost. A number like $180 is abstract enough to be pulled around by whatever it's compared against. But $180 for a coat you'll wear maybe twenty times this winter comes out to nine dollars a wear. That's concrete in a way that resists comparison tricks, because it's now measured against your actual life instead of against some other number someone chose for you. Do this with anything that has a real anchor attached — the gym membership becomes a cost per visit, the subscription becomes a cost per use, the mattress becomes a cost per night over its expected life. Anchors work on abstract prices. They lose most of their grip on prices you've already translated into your own terms.

Gather multiple independent anchors before trusting any single one. Because a single overheard number — from a friend, a colleague, a review — can anchor you just as effectively as a price tag, deliberately collect several independent reference points before treating any of them as reliable. Three or four genuinely separate data points give you an actual range to reason from; a single one, no matter how confidently it was delivered, is just one more gravity well waiting to pull your judgment somewhere it might not belong.

Restate every price back in its full-commitment form before deciding, and say the number out loud. Whichever direction the framing trick runs — a large number broken into a deceptively small daily unit, or a small number left unexamined at its sticker-price scale — the simple discipline of saying the full, honest commitment out loud to yourself before deciding does more to break the anchor's grip than silent mental math ever does, because hearing the number spoken engages a different, more deliberate mode of evaluation than glancing past it on a screen.

Ask the cash question. If someone handed you the full amount in cash right now, with no tag, no markdown, no comparison anywhere in sight, would you choose to spend it on this specific thing? Not "is this a good deal" — deals are relative, and relative is exactly the trap. Just: given this money, free of any anchor, is this where it goes? If the honest answer is a clear yes, the anchor was irrelevant anyway and you can buy without a second thought. If the answer is a hesitant yes or a no, that hesitation is the anchor's fingerprints — you weren't drawn to the thing, you were drawn to the gap between two numbers, and the gap isn't yours to keep once you walk out with the thing itself.

The rule to remember: *The first number you see isn't information about the thing — it's a lever on your judgment. Bring your own number before you let someone else bring* *theirs.*

Chapter 6 — The Scarcity Brain

Why having more rarely feels like having enough

There's a specific kind of tired that has nothing to do with sleep. It's the tired of doing the math again — the same math you did last week, and the week before, moving the same numbers around in your head, trying to make them land somewhere safer than they currently sit. You've done this math so many times you could do it walking, talking, half-asleep. And here's the strange part, the part that doesn't make sense from the outside: doing it again doesn't actually change the numbers. You already know the answer before you start. You do it anyway, because not doing it feels more dangerous than doing it uselessly for the hundredth time.

This is what it feels like to think from inside scarcity, and it isn't the same thing as poverty, though it's related to it. Scarcity is a *state of mind*, and it can attach itself to money at almost any income, because what triggers it isn't the size of the number in your account. It's the felt distance between what you have and what you need to feel safe — and for a lot of people, no matter how that distance narrows on paper, it never quite narrows in the part of the mind that's doing the constant math.

There's a version of this that shows up specifically around time rather than money, which is worth naming because it reveals how general the underlying mechanism actually is: someone whose calendar is genuinely overbooked can develop the exact same tunneling response toward their schedule that a financially scarce person develops toward their bank balance — constantly recalculating, unable to think clearly about anything outside the immediate crunch, saying yes to things reflexively because the tunnel doesn't have bandwidth left to properly weigh a no. Mullainathan and Shafir's research specifically found that scarcity of time produces measurably similar cognitive effects to scarcity of money, which tells you this was never really a "money psychology" phenomenon in the first place. It's a general response to felt insufficiency of any critical resource, and money is simply the version that happens to be the subject of this book.

You notice it most clearly in the moments it doesn't belong. A friend offers to split a bill evenly though you ordered less, and something in you tightens before you've even decided whether to say anything. A small unexpected expense arrives — nothing catastrophic, just unplanned — and the reaction is wildly out of proportion to the actual dollar amount, because the mind isn't really responding to this specific number. It's responding to what this number represents: one more thing pulling at a margin that already feels too thin, regardless of what the margin actually measures out to on paper.

It shows up in a very different room too, one with no shortage of money in it at all: the negotiation over a raise, a promotion, a rate increase for freelance work. Someone underpaid for years, whose scarcity mindset was installed by a genuinely lean period, can find themselves unable to ask for what the market would clearly support, not because they don't know their own worth intellectually, but because the tunnel installed during the lean years still runs the calculation as if any request might tip the whole precarious system over. They'll accept a below-market offer that a colleague with an identical resume and a differently-calibrated history would reject without a second thought — the difference isn't skill, or leverage, or even confidence in the ordinary sense. It's which version of "normal" each of their minds is quietly running the math against.

What's actually happening

Researchers who study scarcity — the economist Sendhil Mullainathan and the psychologist Eldar Shafir did some of the defining work on this — found something that reframes the whole subject: scarcity isn't just an emotional state that makes you anxious. It's a *cognitive* state, meaning it actually changes how much working mental capacity you have available for everything else. Their research compared this to a kind of mental bandwidth tax. When a mind is preoccupied with not having enough, it doesn't just feel worse — it gets measurably worse at unrelated tasks, because a portion of its processing power is permanently allocated to the scarcity itself, running in the background, all the time, whether you're actively worrying or not.

Here's the part that reframes almost everything: scarcity creates *tunneling* — a narrowing of attention onto the scarce resource, at the cost of everything outside the tunnel. If you're short on money, your mind becomes extremely, almost supernaturally good at solving the immediate money problem in front of you — and correspondingly worse at everything just outside that tunnel's edge. The long-term plan. The preventive step that would cost a little now to save a lot later. The opportunity that doesn't scream for attention the way the immediate shortfall does. None of this is a character flaw. It's what a mind under scarcity is *built* to do — focus hard on the urgent gap, because in a genuine emergency, tunnel vision is exactly the right tool. The trouble is that the tunnel doesn't know the difference between a real emergency and a chronic, ongoing state, and it stays open indefinitely if the felt shortage never resolves.

And this is where the trap for a scarcity mindset gets cruel: the mindset can persist long after the actual shortage has eased. If you spent formative years, or even just a rough stretch of adult life, in a real state of not-enough, your mind can get calibrated there — the tunnel becomes the default operating mode, and it doesn't automatically widen back out just because your income eventually does. You can be, by any external measure, financially fine, and still run every decision through the same tight, urgent, not-enough calculation your mind learned to run when it actually was in danger. The math changes. The felt danger doesn't, not on its own.

There's a physiological layer worth naming too, because it explains why scarcity thinking feels so distinctly *bodily* and not just cognitive: chronic financial stress activates the same stress-response systems that respond to physical threat, keeping cortisol and related stress hormones elevated over extended periods rather than the brief spikes those systems were designed to handle. A body running in this state isn't just anxious in an abstract sense — it's operating with genuinely altered sleep, altered appetite, altered immune function, all downstream of a threat system that doesn't distinguish between a predator and a persistently tight bank balance. This is part of why scarcity thinking is so exhausting in ways that go beyond the mental math: the body is quietly paying a physical cost for a threat state that, in the ancestral environment, was never meant to run for months or years at a stretch.

There's a second layer worth naming honestly, because it explains why "just relax about money" is such useless advice: scarcity thinking also *produces* some of the very outcomes that then confirm it. A mind narrowed onto the immediate gap is, by the research, worse at the kind of patient, big-picture financial planning that actually closes gaps over time — not because the person is bad with money, but because the tunnel makes long-horizon thinking expensive in a moment when the mind's resources are already spoken for. So the scarcity produces short-term thinking, the short-term thinking produces exactly the kind of decisions that keep the gap open, and the open gap keeps the scarcity mindset justified. It isn't a personal failing feeding itself. It's a cognitive tax feeding itself.

There's a further piece worth naming from psychologist Richard Lazarus's research on stress and coping, which distinguishes between two very different responses once a threat is appraised: problem-focused coping, which acts directly on the source of the stress, and emotion-focused coping, which manages the *feeling* of the stress without necessarily changing its source. Scarcity thinking pushes people, disproportionately, toward the emotion-focused mode — the anxious re-checking, the mental rehearsal, the doing-the-math-again described at the top of this chapter — precisely because the tunnel narrows attention onto the felt danger rather than onto the structural moves that would actually resolve it. This is why "just think positive" advice fails so completely here: it's not offering a real problem-focused alternative, just a different, equally unhelpful emotion-focused strategy. The actual answer has to be structural, which is exactly what the overrides below are built to be.

What it costs you

The direct cost is the one you already feel: a level of chronic low-grade dread around money that doesn't fully lift even when the actual numbers improve, because the mindset and the numbers aren't the same thing and don't move on the same schedule.

The deeper cost is what the tunnel takes from everything just outside it. Relationships strained by a preoccupation you can't fully explain or set down, even in moments meant for something else. Health, because the mental bandwidth that would go toward a doctor's appointment or a better meal or consistent sleep is already spent on the scarce resource, whatever it is. Opportunities that required patient, wide-lens thinking — the kind the tunnel doesn't have room for — passed over in favor of whatever solves the most urgent thing in front of you today. None of this shows up as a line item. It shows up as a life that stays smaller than the numbers alone would explain, because the tunnel, once installed, doesn't check your bank balance before deciding how much room it needs.

There's a family-systems version of this cost worth naming, because scarcity thinking rarely stays contained to the person experiencing it directly. A parent running a chronic scarcity tunnel, even a mild one, tends to transmit the underlying calibration to their children — not through any explicit lesson, but through the thousand small, absorbed cues of how money gets discussed, flinched at, and reacted to around the house. A child who grows up watching a parent do the anxious re-checking described at the top of this chapter often absorbs the felt sense that money is dangerous and scarce, sometimes regardless of the family's actual financial position, which is part of why scarcity mindsets can persist for a full generation past the actual conditions that originally produced them.

There's a specific irony worth naming about how scarcity thinking interacts with actual financial opportunity, because it can quietly sabotage the exact moves that would resolve it. Tunneling makes patient, research-heavy decisions — comparing loan terms, researching a better financial product, taking the time to understand an investment option properly — disproportionately expensive in terms of available mental bandwidth, which means people already under scarcity pressure are systematically pushed toward the fastest available option rather than the best one, even when the best one would have cost nothing extra to access. The payday loan chosen over a slower, cheaper alternative; the first insurance plan encountered rather than the one that would have actually fit better — none of this reflects worse judgment in any general sense. It reflects a tunnel that has made the *research itself* feel like an expense the person can't currently afford, even when the research would have saved them money in the end.

There's also a quieter cost that's easy to miss because it looks like the opposite of scarcity: the version of this pattern that shows up in people who have plenty, on paper, but never feel like they do. The tunnel doesn't require an actual shortage to run. It requires a felt distance between what you have and what you've decided constitutes "enough" — and if "enough" was never defined, that distance can persist at almost any income, because the finish line keeps moving to stay just out of reach. This is scarcity's stranger cousin: not the tunnel of true shortage, but a tunnel built entirely out of an undefined target, running the same anxious math on numbers that, to almost anyone watching from outside, would already look like enough.

The overrides

You can't think your way out of a cognitive tax through willpower alone — the tunnel isn't a mood, it's a resource allocation, and resource allocations respond to structure, not to being told to relax.

Build in a deliberate research buffer for major decisions. Because tunneling makes the research step itself feel unaffordable, pre-commit to a fixed amount of comparison time — even just thirty minutes — before any decision above a threshold you choose, treating that time as non-negotiable rather than something to skip when the tunnel is at its narrowest. This directly counters the finding that scarcity pushes people toward the fastest option rather than the best one, by making the slower option's first step small enough to survive the bandwidth tax.

Write down your actual enough number. Most scarcity-driven anxiety runs on an undefined target, which means there's no number that could ever satisfy it — the tunnel just keeps narrowing regardless of what you have, because it was never told what the finish line was. So define it, on paper, specifically: what number, in savings, in monthly income, in whatever form matters to you, would constitute genuinely enough — not aspirational, not impressive, just *enough* to stop the emergency-mode math. Once that number exists on paper, your mind has something concrete to check progress against, instead of an open-ended, ever-receding sense of not-there-yet. People are frequently startled, doing this exercise honestly, to find their enough number is smaller than the number their anxiety has been running against.

Widen the lens specifically on time, not just money, when the tunnel feels active. If you notice the narrowed, urgent, constantly-recalculating quality of scarcity thinking but your bank balance genuinely isn't the issue, check your calendar with the same scrutiny you'd give a budget. An overcommitted schedule can trigger the identical tunnel, and the fix — saying no to something, freeing a block of unscheduled time — is structurally the same override as freeing up a financial margin, just applied to a different resource entirely.

Batch the worry into a scheduled window. The tunnel wants to run constantly, in the background, stealing bandwidth from everything else. Give it a specific, bounded time instead — fifteen minutes, once a week, where you're allowed to do the math as thoroughly and anxiously as you want. Outside that window, when the worry tries to surface, the rule is simple: it goes on the list for the scheduled time, not into this moment. This doesn't make the worry disappear. It contains it, which is different and, for a resource-allocation problem, more effective — you're not fighting the tunnel, you're giving it a smaller box to live in so the rest of your mind gets its bandwidth back for the other twenty-three hours and forty-five minutes of the day.

Notice when the tunnel has migrated to a different resource. If money feels less scarce than it used to but the same narrowed, anxious, constantly-recalculating feeling persists, check whether the tunnel has simply relocated to time, energy, or attention rather than actually resolving. Because the underlying mechanism is general-purpose, treating a time-scarcity tunnel with money-focused interventions won't touch it — the fix has to target whichever resource is actually triggering the tunneling right now, not just the one this chapter happens to be about.

Take an honest abundance inventory. Because tunneling narrows attention specifically onto the scarce thing, it's very good at hiding evidence that would contradict it. Once, deliberately, widen the lens: what do you actually have — savings, skills, relationships, options — that the tunnel's narrow focus has been keeping out of view? This isn't a gratitude exercise for its own sake. It's a direct counter to a cognitive mechanism that systematically underweights everything outside the gap. Seeing the full picture, even briefly, can loosen a tunnel that's been running on incomplete information for a long time.

The rule to remember: *Scarcity is a tunnel, not a truth. Define your enough number, and you give the tunnel something to finally stop running against.*

Chapter 7 — The Worst-Time Reflex

Why your brain makes you sell, quit, or run at exactly the wrong moment

The market drops. Not gently — the kind of drop that shows up on the news, the kind your phone lights up about, the kind where every account you check is red. And somewhere in your chest, before you've consciously decided anything, there's already a pull toward one single action: get out. Sell it. Stop the bleeding. It doesn't feel like a financial decision. It feels like pulling your hand off a hot stove — instant, correct, not up for debate.

Here's what almost never gets said in the moment: that instinct, the one that feels so obviously right, is disproportionately the instinct that's about to cost you the most. Not always — sometimes the hand really is on a hot stove, and getting out really is correct. But far more often than the reflex would have you believe, the moment that feels most urgently like an emergency is the exact moment your mind is least equipped to make the call, because the reflex driving the urgency wasn't built for portfolios. It was built for something much older and much more literal.

The same reflex shows up quieter, away from markets entirely, in decisions that never make the news. A difficult stretch in a business, a hard season in a job, a training program that's gotten harder before it's gotten easier — each one can produce the identical chest-tightening pull toward immediate exit, dressed up as clarity rather than panic. "I finally see this clearly" is what the reflex tells you, in the exact voice of genuine insight, right as it's doing its least clear thinking of the entire process.

The same reflex has a quieter, slower-motion cousin that never makes headlines because it doesn't happen in a single dramatic moment: the years-long avoidance of a category of decision entirely, because a single bad experience once produced the panic-exit response and the mind generalized from it. Someone who sold in a panic during one downturn, taking a real loss, can spend the next decade essentially locked out of investing altogether — not through a conscious, considered decision that investing isn't for them, but through a nervous system that filed the entire category under "dangerous" after one bad exit, and never got the update that the danger was the exit, not the category. The cost of that kind of avoidance rarely gets counted, because it never shows up as a loss on any statement. It shows up as growth that simply never happened, for years, to money that sat in cash out of a fear that was never re-examined after the moment that installed it.

What's actually happening

The mechanism underneath this has a name in behavioral economics — loss aversion — and it comes from research by the same Daniel Kahneman, working with Amos Tversky, that gave us the anchor. Their finding, now one of the most replicated results in the field: losses and gains of the same size are not felt as equal and opposite. Losing a given amount hurts measurably more than gaining that same amount feels good. Not slightly more. In their original estimates, something in the range of twice as much, though the exact multiple varies by context and person. Your brain isn't a neutral calculator weighing gains against losses on a level scale. It has its thumb on the scale, and the thumb presses down hard on the loss side.

There's a specific detail from the original research worth knowing, because it shows how consistent this asymmetry is across contexts most people wouldn't expect it to apply to: Kahneman and Tversky's prospect theory findings held up not just for money but across a wide range of decisions involving risk, from medical choices to insurance to simple gambles, suggesting the loss-aversion machinery isn't a money-specific quirk bolted onto an otherwise rational financial brain. It's a general-purpose feature of how humans weigh outcomes, wherever the outcomes can be framed as a gain or a loss relative to some reference point — which means the market-panic reflex covered in this chapter and the medical-decision anxieties, insurance over-purchasing, and general risk-aversion many people experience in completely different areas of life are, structurally, downstream of the identical asymmetry, just triggered by different categories of threat.

Why would a mind be built this asymmetrically? Because for almost all of human history, a loss and a gain were not actually equivalent in survival terms. A gain — more food, more resources, a bit of extra safety — was nice to have. A loss — of food, of safety, of standing — could be the difference between making it through the season and not. A mind that weighted losses more heavily than equivalent gains wasn't being irrational. It was correctly pricing in a world where losses were disproportionately dangerous compared to gains. The asymmetry is a feature, inherited from an environment where it kept people alive.

The trouble, as with almost everything in this book, is the modern mismatch. A market drop registers, to the ancient part of your brain running this calculation, as a *loss event* — and loss events trigger a threat response, not a considered one. The same physiological machinery that would have you drop what you're doing and act, fast, in the face of a genuine physical danger gets recruited by a red number on a screen. Your heart rate actually changes. Your available thinking narrows, the same tunneling effect from scarcity, now triggered by a single sharp event instead of a chronic state. And the action that threat response wants, overwhelmingly, is to *do something* — to stop the loss, right now, by any means available. In a genuine physical emergency, that reflex saves you. In a market downturn, the action it produces — selling at the bottom, in a state of narrowed, threat-driven urgency — is very often the single most expensive decision available at that moment, and it's the one the reflex is built to push you toward hardest.

There's a mirror-image version of this reflex that gets far less attention but does comparable damage: the euphoric buy-in at exactly the wrong moment, driven by the same threat-response machinery running in reverse. A sharp, fast gain can trigger an urgency response just as strong as a sharp loss — a fear of missing out that produces the identical narrowed, threat-driven, act-now cognitive state, just aimed at buying instead of selling. The person who watches an asset spike and feels compelled to buy in immediately, right at the top, before it "gets away from them," is running the exact same tunneled, reflexive machinery as the panic-seller at the bottom. Both are convinced, in the moment, that they're finally seeing clearly. Both are, more often than not, making the decision at precisely the moment their judgment is least trustworthy.

This isn't confined to markets. The same reflex fires when a business idea hits a rough patch and the urge is to shut it down immediately, right when patience was the actual answer. It fires in a job that's become difficult, pushing toward a hasty exit before a better option exists, driven by the same loss-triggered urgency rather than a clear-eyed read of the situation. Anywhere a felt loss creates a sense of emergency, the same machinery activates, and the action it produces is optimized for a world of physical threats, not one of financial ones — where the correct move is very often to do nothing at all, at least not yet, and the reflex has almost no capacity to tolerate that answer.

There's an additional mechanism worth naming, from psychologist Leon Festinger again, though from an entirely different piece of his work than the social-comparison research cited in an earlier chapter: cognitive dissonance, the discomfort that arises when a belief and an action, or two beliefs, conflict with each other, and the mind's strong pull to resolve that discomfort — often by changing the belief rather than by confronting the harder truth. Someone who sells at the bottom in a panic and then watches the market recover faces exactly this kind of dissonance: "I am a reasonably sensible person" collides with "I just made an obviously bad, fear-driven decision."

Rather than sit with that collision, the mind often resolves it by retroactively rewriting the story — "the market was going to keep falling, I got out just in time, I was right to be cautious" — a revision that feels better in the moment but actively prevents the kind of honest post-mortem that would help the same reflex get caught earlier next time. The dissonance doesn't just distort the decision. It distorts the memory of the decision afterward, which is part of why the same reflex tends to recur across a person's financial life instead of being learned from.

What it costs you

The direct, measurable cost shows up starkly in long-run data on investor behavior: people who move their money in and out chasing the market's swings, driven by exactly this reflex, systematically underperform people who simply hold steady through the same period — not because the movers are less intelligent or less informed, but because the decisions get made at the worst possible moments, when the threat response is loudest and the thinking is narrowest. The sell happens near the bottom, when the loss feels most urgent. The buy-back happens after the recovery is already underway, when the fear has faded enough to let you back in — which means you've paid, structurally, for the exact wrong side of both moves, over and over, driven by a reflex that has no way of knowing it's wrong in the moment it's firing.

There's a specific version of this cost worth naming in the context of retirement accounts, where the structural design of the account itself can either protect against or expose someone to the reflex. Accounts that make it easy to view balances daily and easy to move money between holdings with a single tap put the reflex in near-constant contact with its trigger; accounts that require more friction to check and more friction to reallocate structurally protect the holder from acting on the reflex even in a moment of genuine panic, simply because the extra steps buy time for the threat response to fade before it can complete its damage. This is worth knowing not because you should seek out clunky, inconvenient financial tools for their own sake, but because the ease of access that gets marketed as a feature is, for this specific pattern, sometimes closer to a liability, and it's worth weighing deliberately rather than defaulting to whichever option is most frictionless.

The less obvious cost is what this reflex does outside of markets specifically — to any long-horizon commitment that has a rough stretch built into it, which is to say, almost all of them. The business that would have worked, given another six months, but got shut down in a moment of loss-triggered panic. The relationship, the training, the slow-building skill, abandoned at exactly the low point that would, in hindsight, have been the wrong moment to quit — not because quitting is always wrong, but because the decision got made by the threat response instead of by a clear read of the actual situation. The reflex doesn't distinguish between "this specific thing is genuinely failing" and "this normally-good thing is having a bad stretch." It just registers loss, and pushes for exit, regardless of which one is actually true.

The overrides

You cannot out-feel a threat response in the moment it's firing — by the time you're in it, the tunneling has already narrowed your available thinking, and reasoning your way out from inside it is exactly as hard as it sounds. The fix has to happen before the moment arrives.

Add friction to your own access, deliberately. Because ease of access keeps the reflex in near-constant contact with its trigger, consider whether the financial tools you use daily make reallocation a single, frictionless tap or a more deliberate, multi-step process. Where you have the choice, favor the version with more friction for anything long-horizon — not because friction is virtuous in itself, but because a few extra steps between impulse and action is often enough time for a threat response to fade before it can complete the damage it was pushing you toward.

Write the decision before the fear does. For any long-horizon commitment where you know a rough patch is likely — an investment plan, a business, anything with a real time horizon — decide, in advance, in a calm moment, exactly what would constitute a real reason to exit, and write it down in specific, checkable terms. Not a feeling. A criterion. When the rough patch arrives and the reflex is screaming for action, your job isn't to decide fresh, in the worst possible mental state to decide in — it's to check the current situation against the criteria your calm self already wrote. Calm-you and threat-you are, functionally, different decision-makers. Let calm-you make the call in advance, and give threat-you a checklist instead of a blank page.

Apply the same brake to euphoric urgency as to panic. Because the fear-of-missing-out reflex runs on the identical threat machinery as the panic-sell, treat any "I need to act immediately or I'll miss this" feeling with the same suspicion, regardless of whether the emotion driving it is excitement or dread. If a decision feels too urgent to sleep on, that urgency is itself diagnostic information — genuinely good opportunities can typically survive a day of calm evaluation; the ones that supposedly can't are disproportionately the ones the reflex, not your judgment, is pushing you toward.

Zoom out further than the reflex wants to. The threat response is built for the immediate, and it will always want to evaluate the situation on the shortest possible timeframe — today's number, this week's news. Deliberately force a wider lens: what does this look like on a ten-year view, not a ten-day one? Most sharp losses that feel like emergencies shrink dramatically in significance once measured against a long enough horizon, and the deliberate act of zooming out is often enough, on its own, to loosen the tunnel's grip, because it reintroduces exactly the context the threat response is built to exclude.

Pre-decide your response to a euphoric spike, not just a panicked one. Write down, in the same calm moment you write your loss-driven exit criteria, what would actually justify buying into a fast-moving opportunity — specific, checkable conditions, not a feeling of excitement or urgency. When the euphoric version of the reflex fires, you'll have the same kind of calm-you checklist to check against that the panic version gets, instead of letting threat-you make either call from inside the tunnel.

Remove the moment from your own hands where you can. The single most reliable defense against a threat-driven decision is to make sure there's no decision to make in the heat of the moment at all. Automate the contribution, the commitment, the plan, so that the default behavior during a rough patch is *continuing* rather than requiring an active choice to stay the course. A reflex can only override a decision that's actually being made live. If the system is already running on autopilot, the reflex has nothing to grab onto.

Audit your past panics for what they actually taught you. If a previous loss-driven exit is quietly steering your decisions years later, find it and look at it directly, on paper, with the dissonance-driven story set aside. What actually happened, in sequence, with real numbers, not the retroactively tidied version? Most people find, once they do this honestly, that the reflex cost them more than the original loss did — the panic-sell was expensive, but the decade of avoidance that followed it was often far more expensive, in growth that never had a chance to happen. Naming that clearly is often enough to loosen a generalization that's been running unexamined for years.

The rule to remember: *The moment that feels most like an emergency is often the moment your judgment is least trustworthy. Decide in advance, so the worst version of you only has to follow instructions, not make the call.*

Chapter 8 — The Unopened Envelope

Why looking at the numbers can feel worse than not knowing them

There's a specific kind of not-knowing that isn't really about information. You could find out the number in about ninety seconds — log in, look, done. And yet the app stays closed. The statement stays in its envelope, or its folder, or wherever digital things go to be avoided. Not because the number is genuinely unknowable. Because, somewhere in you, not looking feels safer than looking, even though the not-looking changes nothing about what the number actually is.

This is one of the stranger patterns in the whole book, because on its surface it makes no sense. Knowing your balance can only help you. Not knowing it can't protect you from anything real — the money is either there or it isn't, whether or not you check. And yet almost everyone has done this at some point: let a bill sit unopened, let an account go unchecked for longer than they'd admit out loud, felt a small flinch of relief in choosing not to look. The relief is real, even though the protection it offers is not. That gap — real relief, fake protection

— is the whole pattern.

There's a version of this that shows up specifically around tax season or annual reviews, where the avoidance compounds because it becomes attached to a recurring deadline rather than a single dreaded task. Someone who puts off gathering their documents until the last possible week, year after year, isn't simply procrastinating on paperwork — they're often avoiding a once-a-year confrontation with a full financial picture that the rest of the year lets them keep comfortably fragmented. Each January the avoidance resets, and each year the eventual confrontation, compressed into a stressful final week, feels more high-stakes than it would have if the same information had simply been reviewed gradually across the preceding months. The deadline doesn't cause the avoidance. It just gives the avoidance a predictable, recurring shape.

It rarely announces itself as avoidance. It shows up disguised as being busy, as meaning to get to it, as a task that keeps sliding down an ever-growing list without ever quite reaching the top, month after month, in a way that would be almost funny if it weren't costing something real. Ask someone mid-avoidance why they haven't looked and they'll give you a logistics answer — time, forgetfulness, a busy week — that doesn't quite explain why the ninety-second task never once made it to the top of a list with plenty of far less urgent things on it.

It shows up in couples in a specific, painful variation: one partner avoiding a joint account statement not because they don't care, but because looking together means the bad news, if there is any, becomes shared and confirmed in front of the one person whose opinion matters most — turning a private anxiety into a witnessed one. Ask around and you'll find plenty of otherwise functional, communicative couples with an unspoken agreement to simply not look closely at certain shared numbers together, an agreement neither of them made out loud, that exists purely because looking together raises the stakes of the anxiety-management calculation described above. It's the same mechanism as the solo unopened envelope, with an extra layer: not just "what if I find out something bad," but "what if we find out something bad, together, and there's no controlling how the other person reacts to it."

What's actually happening

The mechanism here isn't really about money at all. It's about anxiety management, and money just happens to be one of the places it shows up most reliably. When a piece of information carries the possibility of bad news, your mind runs a quiet cost-benefit calculation that has nothing to do with logic: right now, in this moment, I don't know, and not-knowing keeps a range of possibilities open, including good ones. If I look, one specific reality gets locked in, and it might be the bad one. Avoidance, in this light, isn't laziness or denial in the simple sense. It's a bid to keep the anxiety at a *known, tolerable level* — the discomfort of not knowing — rather than risk it spiking to a potentially much higher level: the discomfort of confirmed bad news.

There's a version of this avoidance that shows up specifically around debt, where the unopened envelope becomes an unopened collections letter, and the stakes of not-looking climb accordingly. The instinct is identical — not looking keeps the range of possibilities open, including the possibility, however unlikely, that it's not as bad as feared — but the consequences of sustained avoidance are considerably steeper, because debt-related avoidance tends to trigger the exact structural costs described later in this chapter faster and more severely than simple balance-checking avoidance does: late fees compound, statute-of-limitations windows on certain debts pass without the protective actions that could have been taken during them, and options that were available early in the process quietly close as the avoidance continues. The mind isn't calculating any of this while it avoids. It's still just running the same anxiety-management trade it always runs, blind to the fact that this particular version of not-looking has a much steeper price tag attached to the waiting.

This is a real trade the mind is making, and it's worth taking seriously rather than just labeling it a flaw. Uncertainty, held at a low simmer, is genuinely more bearable, moment to moment, than a confirmed problem — even though the confirmed problem is often more manageable in the long run, precisely because you can actually do something about a known number that you can't do about an unknown one. The mind is optimizing for the next five minutes of felt safety, not for the actual trajectory of your finances, because that's what anxiety-management systems are built to do. They protect you from the feeling, not from the underlying reality — and money problems are one of the few kinds of danger where the feeling and the reality can be pried apart for a surprisingly long time before they catch back up to each other.

There's a specific version of this worth naming that shows up around insurance and warranty documents, a category of unopened envelope that's easy to overlook because the avoidance there doesn't even feel like avoidance — it feels like reasonable disinterest in paperwork nobody enjoys reading. But the same anxiety-management logic runs underneath: not reading the policy carefully means not confronting exactly what isn't covered, which keeps a vague, comfortable sense of "I'm probably fine" intact for as long as the document stays unread. The cost of this particular version of avoidance often stays completely invisible until the exact moment it matters most — a claim gets filed, a gap in coverage is discovered for the first time, and the unread document turns out to have been telling a very different story than the comfortable assumption was.

There's a specific way this compounds that makes it worse over time rather than better: every day the envelope stays unopened, the imagined version of what's inside tends to get worse, not more accurate. In the absence of real information, your mind doesn't default to a neutral guess — it tends to fill the gap with the worst plausible version, because a threat-management system errs toward assuming danger rather than assuming safety. So the longer the avoidance runs, the more frightening the imagined number becomes, which makes the actual number — however bad it might be — feel like an even bigger risk to confirm, which extends the avoidance further. The gap between the feared number and the real one, in most cases, turns out to be enormous once someone finally looks. But that gap can only close by looking, and looking is the exact thing the anxiety-management system is built to prevent.

There's also an identity layer worth naming honestly, because it often runs underneath the anxiety and makes the avoidance stickier. For a lot of people, checking the number doesn't just risk finding out something is wrong — it risks confirming something about *who they are*: someone who's bad with money, someone who's behind, someone who let this happen. The avoidance isn't just protecting them from a number. It's protecting a self-image from a piece of evidence that might contradict it. That's a harder thing to override than simple anxiety, because it isn't really about the money at all — it's about which story you get to keep telling about yourself, and looking threatens to end that story on someone else's terms.

There's a related mechanism worth naming from psychologist Dan Kahan's research on what's sometimes called identity-protective cognition — the finding that people process threatening information differently depending on whether accepting it would require revising a piece of their self-concept, often unconsciously distorting or avoiding information that conflicts with the identity they're invested in. Applied here, this deepens the identity layer already touched on: it's not simply that looking might confirm bad news, but that looking might force a specific, identity-level admission — "I am someone who is behind," "I am someone who let this happen" — that the mind will go to real lengths to avoid, including simply not gathering the information that would force the admission in the first place.

This is why the avoidance can persist even in people who are otherwise highly capable, organized, and on top of everything else in their lives. It was never really about capability. It was about protecting a self-concept from a specific category of evidence.

What it costs you

The direct cost compounds silently, because problems that go unmonitored tend to get worse rather than stay static — a small, manageable gap can grow into a much larger one purely through the passage of unattended time, and the avoidance guarantees that time passes with nobody watching. Fees accrue. Small fixable issues become larger ones. Opportunities to course-correct early, when correction is cheap and easy, quietly expire while the envelope stays closed.

There's a specific way this avoidance interacts with debt collection processes worth naming honestly, because it's one of the clearest places where the cost of not-looking becomes structurally, legally concrete rather than just emotionally corrosive. Many debt-related processes have specific windows during which a person has meaningfully more options — to negotiate, to dispute, to set up a manageable arrangement — than they do once those windows close and the matter proceeds further along its default track. Avoidance doesn't just delay the emotional reckoning in these cases. It can quietly forfeit options that were only available during a window the avoidance ran straight through, unopened, unread, unaddressed. This is the sharpest version of "not looking doesn't protect you" in the entire chapter: in this specific context, not looking can convert a solvable problem into a considerably harder one, purely through the passage of unattended time.

The deeper cost is what chronic avoidance does to your relationship with your own financial life. Every day you don't look, you reinforce, a little more, the belief that looking is dangerous — which makes the next day's avoidance easier to justify and the eventual look feel even higher-stakes than it did before. You end up governed by a number you've never confirmed, making decisions in its imagined shadow rather than its actual light, and the imagined shadow, as established, tends to be worse than the truth. This is its own kind of tax: you pay the emotional cost of a crisis you haven't confirmed is even real, for as long as the avoidance holds.

The overrides

You cannot argue your way past an anxiety-management system with logic alone — it isn't running on logic, it's running on felt safety, and it needs a different kind of intervention.

Read insurance and warranty documents once, deliberately, before you need them. Set aside a specific, bounded time to actually read the coverage documents you're currently avoiding — not searching for reassurance, just building an accurate picture of what is and isn't covered while there's no active claim creating pressure. This converts a potentially catastrophic surprise, discovered at the worst possible moment, into a known quantity you can plan around calmly, which is a far cheaper time to absorb bad news than in the middle of an actual emergency.

The five-minute look-without-fixing ritual. The reason looking feels so dangerous is that it's bundled, in your mind, with an obligation to immediately solve whatever you find.

Unbundle them. Give yourself explicit permission to look at the number with zero requirement to do anything about it yet — just look, note what's there, and stop. This sounds like it shouldn't work, but it does, because it's the *fixing* obligation, not the *looking*, that makes the anxiety spike so high. Remove the obligation, and looking becomes a much smaller, much more survivable act — small enough that you can actually do it.

Set a specific date for reading dormant coverage documents. Rather than letting insurance and warranty paperwork join the general pile of avoided financial tasks, give it its own dedicated date on the calendar, separate from the weekly money check-in, since the content and stakes are different enough to deserve their own unhurried, undistracted read-through rather than being squeezed into a five-minute balance check.

Establish a standing weekly money date. A single act of looking helps once. A standing, low-stakes habit of looking changes the entire relationship, because it converts an occasional high-stakes confrontation into a routine, low-stakes check-in — the same way a single dentist visit after years of avoidance is dreadful, but a standing six-month cleaning schedule never builds up enough backlog to be frightening. Pick a specific day, a specific short window, and treat it as non-negotiable but genuinely low-pressure. The goal isn't a deep financial review. It's simply keeping the gap between what you know and what's actually true from ever growing large enough to become frightening again.

Break recurring deadlines into smaller, scheduled check-ins. If the avoidance has attached itself to an annual event like taxes, deliberately convert the once-a-year confrontation into several smaller ones spread across the calendar — a quarterly gathering of documents, say, instead of a single January scramble. This applies the same look-without-fixing and standing-date principles above, but specifically targets the way recurring deadlines let avoidance rebuild itself fresh every single year, undoing whatever progress the previous year's eventual confrontation produced.

Shrink the first look to the smallest possible step. If the full picture feels too large to face, don't start there. Look at one single number — just the checking account balance, nothing else — and let that be the whole task for day one. The anxiety-management system is responding to the size of the perceived confrontation, not the actual content, so a smaller first step genuinely produces a smaller spike of resistance. Once that one number has been looked at and survived, the next one is easier, because you've just proven to the anxious part of your mind that looking didn't produce the catastrophe it was bracing for.

If you're avoiding it as a pair, name the shared rule out loud before you look together. If a partner is involved, agree explicitly, before opening anything, on what happens with whatever you find — no blame assigned in the moment, no decisions demanded on the spot, just a shared look followed by a cooling-off period before either of you has to respond to it. This removes the specific fear driving joint avoidance, which isn't really about the number, it's about being judged in real time for it. A stated rule, agreed in advance while calm, does for a couple what the individual overrides above do for one person: it separates the looking from the immediate obligation to react.

The rule to remember: *Not looking doesn't protect you from the number — it only protects you from knowing it. The number is the same either way; only your ability to do something about it changes.*

Chapter 9 — The Sunk-Cost Trap

Why you keep going, long after it stopped making sense, because you've already spent so much

The subscription hasn't been used in months. The course sits half-finished, its later modules unopened. The struggling investment stays in the account, waiting for a recovery that isn't coming. In every case, if you asked the question fresh — knowing nothing about the past, just looking at where things stand right now — the honest answer would be to stop, to cancel, to sell, to walk away. And in every case, something holds you there anyway. Not hope, exactly, and not even real belief that things will turn around. Something quieter and stranger: the sense that walking away now would mean the money, the time, the effort already spent was *wasted* — and stopping feels like it would make that waste official, permanent, undeniable, in a way that continuing somehow doesn't.

There's a version of the trap that runs on time rather than money, and it can be even harder to walk away from because time, unlike money, can never be recovered under any circumstance, which makes the felt cost of "wasting" it hit even harder. Years spent training for a career path that's clearly stopped fitting, a degree half-finished long after the original motivation for it has faded, a relationship kept going mainly because of how long it's already lasted — in each case, the years already invested exert a pull on the present decision precisely because time feels even more irreversible than money, even though the same logic applies with equal force to both: the years are gone regardless of what happens next, and only the question of what to do from here should carry any weight.

It shows up in far smaller versions too, ones that never rise to the level of a real financial decision but drain something anyway. The meal you keep eating well past being full because you already paid for it. The book you finish out of some sense of obligation to the hours already spent, even once it's clear the rest won't be worth reading. None of these are really about the specific dollars or hours. They're about a mind that has trouble treating a past cost as genuinely, permanently gone, and keeps trying, uselessly, to earn it back through sheer continuation.

Here is the strange logic laid bare, because it rarely gets said out loud: the money is already gone. It was gone the moment you spent it, whether you continue or stop. Nothing about continuing brings it back, and nothing about stopping loses anything you still had. And yet the past spending exerts a pull on the present decision as if it were still somehow retrievable — as if enough additional investment might reach back in time and un-waste what's already spent. It can't. That's not how any of this works. But the pull is real, and it's one of the most reliably documented patterns in how people actually make decisions, as opposed to how they'd make decisions if they were coldly rational.

It shows up with particular intensity in small businesses, where the sunk cost isn't just money but years — and the years make the trap far harder to escape than any purely financial version of it. An owner who has put a decade into a business that stopped being viable two years ago will often keep going, drawing down savings, taking on debt, working punishing hours, long after any fresh analysis of the current numbers would say to stop. Ask them directly why they're still going and the answer is rarely "because the numbers work." It's some version of "I can't walk away after everything I've put in" —

which is the sunk-cost trap stated almost word for word, except dressed in the language of grit and commitment, which makes it much harder to recognize as the same pattern that keeps someone finishing a bad book or holding a declining stock.

What's actually happening

This is the sunk-cost trap, and the researcher most associated with formalizing how it operates in everyday financial decisions is Richard Thaler, whose work on the gap between how people actually behave and how classical economic models assumed they'd behave helped found an entire field. The core finding: people treat money that's already been spent as if it were still relevant to a forward-looking decision, when, rationally, it isn't. The only thing that should matter for a decision about what to do next is the situation *as it stands now* — what continuing will cost, what it might return, compared to what stopping would free up. What you already spent to get here is, from a purely forward-looking standpoint, irrelevant. It's gone regardless of what you decide next.

There's a version of the sunk-cost trap that shows up specifically in skill acquisition, where the sunk cost is neither pure money nor pure time but a specific, hard-won identity: "I am someone who is good at this," built over years, that becomes difficult to set down even once the skill has stopped being useful or the field has moved on. A professional whose expertise was built around a technology, method, or approach that's since become obsolete will often keep investing in maintaining and defending that expertise long after a fresh evaluation would recommend pivoting, not because the math is unclear but because the sunk cost here isn't measured in dollars — it's measured in identity, and identity is, if anything, harder to write off than money, because there's no equivalent of "the money is already spent" that applies cleanly to years of being known as the person who's good at a particular thing.

But your mind doesn't process it as irrelevant, because of what stopping would mean symbolically. Continuing lets you avoid ever formally acknowledging the spending as a loss — as long as the thing is still technically ongoing, the money spent on it can be filed, quietly, under "investment," something with an open, still-possible outcome. Stopping converts it, instantly and irreversibly, into “loss” — a closed, confirmed category, and confirmed losses, as the previous chapter’s mechanism showed, hit harder than almost anything else in the emotional ledger. So continuing isn’t really a bet on the thing succeeding anymore. It’s a bet on *not having to feel the loss yet* — which is a completely different bet, and a much worse one, because it’s optimizing for delaying a feeling rather than for the actual outcome.

There’s a specific mechanism worth naming from psychologist William Swann’s research on self-verification theory, which adds a layer the identity discussion above only partly covers. This research found that people are motivated not just to feel good about themselves, but specifically to have their existing self-concept *confirmed*, even when that self-concept is negative — a person who already believes they’re “bad with money” can find a strange, uncomfortable comfort in evidence that fits that belief, because confirmation, even unflattering confirmation, feels more coherent and manageable than the disorientation of having a long-held self-concept contradicted.

This complicates the simple story of sunk-cost avoidance as pure identity protection: sometimes continuing a failing venture isn't just about avoiding the label "someone who wastes money" — for a person who already privately holds that label, continuing can perversely feel like the path of least psychological resistance, because it doesn't force a jarring update to a self-concept that's already, quietly, been settled on.

There's a related thread here, tied to identity in the same way the unopened envelope was: quitting can feel like an admission, not just about the specific decision, but about the kind of person you are — someone who wastes money, who doesn't follow through, who made a bad call. Continuing, however illogically, lets that admission stay deferred. This is why sunk-cost decisions are often defended so fiercely, with reasoning that sounds confident on the surface — "I've come this far," "it would be a waste to stop now" — when what's actually happening underneath is much more about protecting a self-image than about the merits of the thing itself.

The trap compounds because every additional dollar or hour spent trying to rescue the sunk cost becomes, itself, a new sunk cost — which then gets weighed into the next version of the same decision, making the pull to continue even stronger than it was before. This is how people end up dramatically over-invested in things that stopped making sense a long time ago: not through one bad decision, but through a long chain of decisions, each one rational-sounding in the moment, each one really just protecting against having to acknowledge the decision before it.

There's a specific reinforcing mechanism worth naming from psychologist Barry Schwartz and others working on commitment and consistency: once a person has publicly stated an intention to continue — told friends about the business, announced the investment, committed out loud to finishing the course — the pressure to remain consistent with that public statement becomes a separate force operating alongside the sunk-cost pull itself, independent of the money already spent. Social psychologists have long documented how strongly people are motivated to appear, and to actually be, consistent with their own prior commitments, especially public ones, because inconsistency carries its own social cost. This means sunk-cost decisions that were made or announced publicly are measurably harder to walk back than identical decisions made privately — not because the underlying math changed, but because a second, independent psychological pressure has stacked on top of the first one, both pointing the same direction: keep going, regardless of what continuing now actually costs.

What it costs you

The direct cost is straightforward and often large: real money and real time, continuing to flow toward something the current facts say isn't worth it, purely to avoid converting a past expenditure into an acknowledged loss that was, in truth, already locked in the moment the money was first spent.

There's a compounding cost worth naming that's specific to relationships and partnerships, where the sunk-cost trap doesn't just cost the individual holding it but everyone downstream of the decision. A business partner, a spouse, a team relying on a shared resource all inherit the consequences of one person's inability to write off a sunk cost — the underperforming joint investment nobody wants to be the one to suggest abandoning, the failing shared venture kept alive past its point of viability because ending it means someone has to be the one who said stop. In these shared contexts, the sunk-cost trap often gets reinforced by a second, social version of itself: nobody wants to be the one who broke the group's collective story of "this is still working," which means the fresh-start reset below has to be run not just individually but explicitly, out loud, with the other people who share the decision.

The deeper cost is opportunity — every dollar and every hour trapped propping up a sunk cost is a dollar and an hour that isn't available for something that might actually be worth continuing. The struggling investment held out of loyalty to its own history is capital that isn't compounding somewhere more promising. The half-finished course, kept technically open so it doesn't count as abandoned, is hours that aren't going toward something you'd actually finish. Sunk-cost thinking doesn't just cost you what you keep spending — it costs you everything that spending could have gone toward instead, for as long as you keep protecting a decision from the past instead of making the best decision available now.

The overrides

You can't dissolve this pattern through sheer willpower, because it isn't really about willpower — it's about which question you're answering, and the trap only works if you keep answering the wrong one.

Name shared sunk costs out loud with everyone who holds them. If a sunk-cost decision involves other people — a partner, a co-founder, a family member — don't run the fresh-start reset silently in your own head and then announce a conclusion. Run it out loud, together, explicitly inviting the other person to answer the same "would you start this today, from zero" question independently before comparing notes. This surfaces the shared-story dynamic directly rather than leaving it to quietly veto whichever individual conclusion either of you privately reached.

The fresh-start reset. For anything you're on the fence about continuing, ask a version of the decision that erases the past entirely: if I didn't already own this, hadn't already spent this, weren't already partway through this — knowing everything I currently know about how it's performing — would

I choose to start it today, from zero? If the honest answer is no, the past spending isn't a reason to continue. It's the reason the question feels harder than it should, and nothing more. This single reframe strips the sunk cost out of the decision almost completely, because it forces the evaluation to run on the current situation instead of on the history attached to it.

Treat sunk time with the same rule as sunk money. Because time-based sunk costs feel even more irreversible than financial ones, and therefore pull even harder, apply the fresh-start reset explicitly to years and hours, not just dollars. If you wouldn't choose to start this path today, from zero, knowing what you now know, the years already spent aren't a reason to continue — they're simply gone, exactly as gone as money already spent, no more retrievable by further continuation than a bad investment is rescued by throwing more capital at it.

Run the stranger test. Imagine handing this exact decision — same numbers, same current trajectory, none of your personal history with it — to a stranger with no emotional stake in the outcome, and asking what they'd do. Strangers aren't protecting a self-image or a past decision; they'll usually see the current math with total clarity, because they have nothing invested in a particular answer. If you can predict, honestly, that a stranger would tell you to stop, that's worth taking seriously — it means your own attachment to the history, not the current facts, is what's keeping you in.

Give identity-based sunk costs their own explicit reckoning. If what's keeping you in isn't money or years but a hard-won professional identity — "I am someone who is good at this" — name that specifically as its own factor, separate from the financial math, and ask directly whether the identity is worth protecting at the price current continuation actually costs. Identities can be rebuilt around new expertise; the years spent defending an outdated one usually cannot be recovered once spent.

Relabel the spending as already gone, because it already is. Part of what keeps the sunk cost alive is language — as long as it's filed under "investment," it still feels retrievable. Deliberately relabel it: this money is spent. Full stop. Not "invested," not "at risk," not "in progress" — spent, past tense, closed. This isn't about self-punishment. It's about giving your mind an accurate category to file the expense under, so the decision about what to do next can be made on today's facts instead of on a lingering hope that continuing might somehow retroactively justify what's already gone.

Separate the public commitment from the private decision. If part of what's keeping you in is the discomfort of walking back something you've told other people, name that pressure explicitly and weigh it as its own, separate factor — not as evidence about whether continuing is actually a good decision. Other people's memory of your announcement fades far faster and matters far less than it feels like it will in the moment of deciding. Most people, asked honestly, can barely recall the specific commitments their friends and colleagues made a year or two ago. The audience keeping you consistent is, once again, mostly imagined.

The rule to remember: *Money already spent has no vote in what happens next. The only question that matters is what you'd choose to do from here, knowing what you know now.*

Chapter 10 — The Endowment Trap

Why the things you already own feel worth more than they actually are

A mug sits on a desk. Ask the person who owns it what they'd sell it for, and they'll name a number. Ask a stranger, looking at the exact same mug with no ownership attached, what they'd pay for it, and their number will almost always be lower — often significantly lower — even though it's the identical object, with identical uses, identical wear, identical everything except one variable: whose hands it happens to be sitting in when the question gets asked.

This isn't a negotiating tactic or a conscious attempt to extract a better price. It's a felt, honest difference in how much the mug seems to be worth, depending entirely on whether you already own it. The moment something becomes yours, its value to you quietly inflates — not because anything about the thing changed, but because ownership itself changes how your mind prices it.

There's a version of the endowment effect that shows up specifically around inherited items, and it's worth naming because the inflation, in this case, isn't really about the object at all. A piece of furniture, a collection, a modest portfolio of investments passed down from a parent or grandparent often carries a felt value far beyond its market price, not because of anything intrinsic to the item, but because parting with it feels like parting with a piece of the relationship it represents. This is the endowment effect at its most understandable and, in a real sense, most legitimate — the felt value here isn't irrational so much as it's measuring something real that simply isn't captured by a market price. The trap isn't in feeling that value. It's in failing to notice when that feeling is quietly overriding a decision — selling a poorly-performing inherited investment, say — that has nothing to do with the relationship and everything to do with whether the money is doing its job.

The effect scales up far beyond mugs, and it gets stronger, not weaker, the longer something has been in your possession. A house lived in for twenty years accumulates a felt value that has little to do with what a neutral market would actually pay for it

— every repair, every memory, every version of yourself that occupied those rooms gets quietly folded into a number that a stranger, walking through with no history attached, would price completely differently. None of that felt value is imaginary or wrong to feel. It's simply not the same thing as market value, and treating the two as interchangeable is where the trap does its real damage.

Consider a version of this that plays out during a home sale, where the endowment effect can cost tens of thousands of dollars in a single decision. A seller who has lived in a house for years, who chose the paint colors, who remembers each room's history, will very often price it meaningfully above what comparable, neutrally-evaluated properties in the same market are actually fetching — not out of greed or poor information, but because the felt value of the house, inflated by years of ownership and memory, has quietly become their honest internal sense of what it's worth. Buyers, who have none of that ownership history, price the exact same structure using a completely different, unencumbered calculation, and the resulting gap — sometimes small, sometimes large enough to leave a house sitting unsold for months — is the endowment effect made visible in one of the highest-stakes transactions most people will ever make.

What's actually happening

This is the endowment effect, and it was demonstrated in exactly this kind of experiment — objects like mugs, handed to one group as owners and priced by another group as potential buyers, with the owners consistently demanding more than the buyers were willing to pay for the same item. It's one of the cleanest illustrations of a broader truth: your mind does not price things on a neutral, absolute scale. It prices them relative to whether you'd be *gaining* them or *losing* them — and losing something you already have registers, thanks to the same loss-aversion asymmetry from the market-panic chapter, as a bigger deal than gaining that same thing would have felt like in the first place.

There's a specific experimental finding worth adding here, because it clarifies just how automatic this mechanism is: follow-up research on the endowment effect found that the gap between selling price and buying price shows up almost immediately after ownership is established — sometimes within minutes of being handed the object — which rules out the simple explanation that the effect is really about accumulated memories or sentimental attachment built up over long possession. Something about the *act* of psychological ownership itself, not the passage of time, triggers the reframing from potential gain to potential loss. This matters practically because it means the endowment effect doesn't require years of history to take hold — it can attach to something you bought an hour ago, which is worth remembering the next time a same-day return or resale feels harder to go through with than the original purchase decision did.

Once you own something, parting with it is coded, by this same asymmetric machinery, as a loss — and losses, as established, hit harder than equivalent gains. So the price you'd need to be paid to give something up climbs above the price you'd have been willing to pay to acquire it in the first place, purely because the transaction has been reframed, by ownership, from a potential gain into a potential loss. Nothing about the object changed. Only which side of the loss-aversion asymmetry you're standing on changed.

There's a version of the endowment effect that operates on ideas and past decisions rather than physical objects, and it's worth naming because it's easy to miss entirely: once you've publicly held a financial opinion, a stock pick, a strategy you recommended to others, that opinion starts to feel like something you own, in almost the same psychological sense as the mug. Evidence that contradicts it gets discounted more heavily than it would if the opinion belonged to someone else, purely because giving up the opinion now registers as a loss of something already possessed, rather than simply updating a belief that never had to be defended in the first place. This is part of why people so often stay loyal to a losing investment thesis well past the point the facts have turned against it — they're not just protecting the money in the position. They're protecting an owned opinion from the specific discomfort of having to let it go.

This mechanism shows up far beyond mugs and garage sales, and it's often invisible precisely because it feels like genuine, considered value rather than a pricing bias. It's the reason a closet full of clothes you haven't worn in years is so hard to let go of, even though you'd never pay today's price to acquire any of them fresh — ownership has already inflated their felt worth past what a neutral buyer would offer. It's the reason canceling a subscription or a service you barely use still produces a flinch of resistance, a sense of giving something up, even when a fresh evaluation would say it was never worth the cost. It's the reason a declining investment is so hard to sell even once the sunk-cost reasoning has been dealt with, because there's a second, separate pull operating alongside it: not just "I already spent this," but "this is mine, and giving it up is a loss, regardless of what I originally paid."

There's a version of the endowment effect worth naming that operates on shared or co-owned assets, where the psychological ownership at stake is collective rather than individual, and the effect can become even harder to override because it now has to clear two separately-endowed minds instead of one. A married couple deciding whether to sell a jointly-owned property, or business partners deciding whether to divest a shared holding, each bring their own version of the endowment inflation to the table, and neither one experiences the other's attachment as fully legitimate, because each person's own inflated valuation feels, from the inside, like simple honest assessment rather than a documented bias. This is part of why shared-asset decisions are so often harder to reach consensus on than the underlying financial facts alone would predict — it isn't necessarily disagreement about the numbers. It's two separate endowment effects, both operating at full strength, colliding.

There's a specific version of this that compounds with the sunk-cost trap rather than replacing it: once you've owned something for a while, both mechanisms run at the same time, each reinforcing the other. The sunk cost says stopping would waste what you spent. The endowment effect says giving it up is a loss, independent of what you spent. Two different, overlapping reasons to hold on, arriving at the same conclusion from two different directions — which is part of why letting go of long-held things, investments, commitments, and possessions alike, can feel disproportionately difficult compared to how hard the decision would be if you encountered the exact same option fresh, with no history and no ownership attached.

There's a related concept from behavioral economists Richard Zeckhauser and William Samuelson worth naming here, because it explains a specific, common variant of the endowment effect that shows up outside of pure ownership: the status quo bias, a documented preference for the current state of affairs simply because it's current, independent of whether it's actually the best available option. Their research found that people disproportionately stick with default options — the retirement plan they were auto-enrolled in, the insurance tier they started with, the bank they've always used — even when a fresh, unbiased comparison would favor switching, purely because the current arrangement carries the psychological weight of being the established baseline. This runs alongside the endowment effect rather than replacing it: you don't just overvalue things you own, you overvalue *arrangements* you're already in, which is why so many people keep paying for a suboptimal financial setup for years past the point where switching would have clearly, measurably served them better.

What it costs you

The direct cost shows up in every transaction where you either overpay to keep something ownership has inflated, or underprice your willingness to walk away from it — money and opportunity sitting locked inside things that are worth less to a neutral evaluator than they feel worth to you, purely as a function of whose hands they're currently in.

There's a version of this cost worth naming specifically around career decisions, where the endowment effect attaches not to a physical object but to a role, a title, a level of seniority already achieved. Someone who has spent years earning a particular position often prices the *idea* of leaving it — even for a genuinely better opportunity elsewhere — using the inflated, ownership-based valuation the endowment effect produces, rather than the valuation a neutral observer comparing the two opportunities fresh would arrive at. This is part of why people frequently stay in roles that have stopped serving them, turning down objectively better offers, not because the math favors staying but because the current role, simply by virtue of being currently held, has quietly become worth more in their own mind than an honest comparison would support.

The deeper cost is what stays cluttered — financially, physically, and otherwise — because the endowment effect makes almost everything you already have feel harder to release than it should. Money sits in underperforming accounts you'd never choose today, because moving it feels like a loss even though staying is the actual loss, compounding quietly. Closets and storage units hold onto possessions worth a fraction of their felt value, taking up space and sometimes money that could go toward something you'd actually use. Commitments — a business partnership, a long-held role, a subscription — persist well past their usefulness, protected by the same quiet inflation that makes anything you already hold feel more valuable than a fresh look would price it at.

The overrides

You can't reason your way past a pricing bias by simply knowing it exists — knowing about the endowment effect doesn't stop the mug's owner from still feeling like it's worth more. The fix has to change the frame the decision is being made inside, not just the facts available to it.

For shared assets, run the reacquisition test separately before comparing. If a possession or investment is jointly held, have each person independently answer the reacquisition question — would I choose to acquire this today, at what it would cost now — before discussing it together. Comparing two independently-generated answers surfaces the gap between each person's endowment inflation far more honestly than a single joint conversation would, where the more attached person's inflation tends to quietly dominate the discussion.

Run the reacquisition test. For anything you're unsure about keeping — a possession, an investment, a subscription, a commitment — ask directly: if I didn't already have this, would I choose to acquire it today, at what it would actually cost me to get it now? This strips out the endowment inflation almost entirely, because it forces the evaluation to run as a fresh acquisition decision rather than a keep-or-lose decision, and those two framings, as established, produce very different numbers for the exact same object.

Try the reverse-price move. Before deciding whether to keep something, imagine you're the neutral buyer instead of the owner — what would you actually offer a stranger for this, knowing nothing except what it is and what condition it's in? That number, not your gut sense of what it's worth to keep, is closer to its real market value. The gap between that number and what you feel it's worth to hold onto is the endowment effect, made visible and measurable instead of invisible and assumed.

Apply the reacquisition test to opinions, not just objects. For a financial belief or strategy you've held and defended for a while, ask the same question you'd ask of a possession: if I encountered this exact position fresh today, with no history of having recommended or held it, would I choose it now? Opinions, like mugs, get endowed the moment you've owned and defended them publicly, and the same reacquisition framing that cuts through possession bias cuts through opinion bias too.

Use the thirty-day box for physical possessions. For things you're unsure about releasing, don't decide immediately — put them somewhere out of sight for thirty days, unavailable but not yet gone. If, at the end of that period, you haven't thought about or missed the item, the felt value was almost entirely the endowment effect rather than genuine ongoing use, and letting go becomes far easier once the illusion has had time to fade on its own, away from the pull of daily visual ownership.

The rule to remember: *Owning something makes it feel more valuable than it is — not because it changed, but because losing it feels worse than never having had it. Price it like a stranger would, not like its owner does.*

Chapter 11 — The Stranger That Is Future You

Why saving feels like giving money away to someone you'll never meet

Ask most people whether they care about their future — their retirement, their older self, the version of them still decades out — and the honest answer is yes, of course, obviously. And yet ask those same people to actually hand over money today, right now, in service of that future self, and something changes. The commitment that felt easy in the abstract becomes strangely hard in the specific, present moment, in a way that doesn't track with how much they claim to care.

There's a reason for that gap, and it isn't hypocrisy. It's that your brain, when it tries to picture your future self, doesn't fully register that person as *you* — not in the same visceral, immediate way it registers the you sitting here right now, with today's wants and today's account balance. Future-you is real in theory. Present-you is real in the felt, urgent sense that actually drives decisions. And when a decision pits a felt, present want against a theoretical, future benefit, the felt thing wins far more often than the math would justify.

There's a version of this that shows up specifically in couples planning a shared future, where each partner's discounting rate can differ enough to become a real source of friction, mistaken for a difference in values when it's actually a difference in how vividly each of them registers their own future self. One partner, whose future self feels concrete and close, pushes for aggressive saving; the other, whose future self feels abstract and distant, experiences the exact same proposal as unreasonable deprivation for no clear reason. Neither is being irresponsible or reckless in any character sense. They're running the identical present-bias mechanism with different underlying calibrations, arguing about a savings rate when the actual disagreement is about how real thirty-years-from-now feels to each of them individually.

Notice how differently this plays out depending on distance. A benefit landing next week can feel almost as real as one landing today — the discounting is mild, the future-self barely feels like a stranger yet. Push that same benefit out to thirty years, and the person receiving it starts to feel less like a future version of you and more like an abstract, unrelated beneficiary you're being asked to fund out of pure obligation. The math of compounding actually rewards patience most heavily at exactly the distance your mind trusts least — which is precisely why this pattern is so expensive and so hard to override through willpower alone.

Watch it show up in a smaller, more frequent decision than retirement saving, and the pattern becomes easier to catch in real time: the choice, made almost daily, between doing a slightly harder thing now that a future version of you would benefit from, and doing the easier thing now that only present-you enjoys. Meal-prepping on Sunday versus ordering out all week. Paying down a balance versus letting it ride at a rate that will cost meaningfully more by the time it's resolved. Each of these, examined honestly, is the exact same present-bias calculation running at a much shorter distance than "retirement," which makes it a useful diagnostic: if you find yourself consistently taking the present-favoring option even at short distances — a week, a month — that's a stronger signal about your baseline discounting rate than any abstract question about how much you claim to care about your future self.

What's actually happening

This tendency has a formal name — present bias, sometimes discussed under the broader umbrella of temporal discounting — and the core finding is simple to state and strange to really absorb: value that's available now is weighted more heavily than the exact same value available later, even when later isn't actually far away, and even when the future amount is objectively larger. Offered a smaller reward today versus a larger reward in a month, plenty of people take the smaller, immediate one — not because they've done the math and decided it's the better deal, but because "now" carries a kind of gravitational pull that "later," however logically superior, simply doesn't match.

There's a specific behavioral finding worth adding, because it shows how much this discounting bends under the shape of the reward rather than staying constant: the size of present bias isn't fixed — it grows sharply for choices involving the very near future and flattens out for choices further out, a pattern researchers sometimes describe as hyperbolic rather than steady discounting. This produces a strange, specific inconsistency: asked to choose between a smaller reward in a year and a larger reward in a year and a month, most people patiently pick the larger, later reward — the one-month gap feels easy to wait through when it's a year away. But offered the exact same one-month gap starting *today* — a smaller reward now versus a larger reward in a month — many of the same people flip and take the smaller, immediate one. The actual time difference is identical in both cases. Only the *distance from today* changed, and that distance alone was enough to flip the decision, which is a precise demonstration of just how much weight "right now" carries that "soon" simply doesn't.

There's research suggesting something even stranger sits underneath this: when people are asked to think about their future selves, the brain activity involved looks, in some studies, more like the pattern associated with thinking about a different person entirely than the pattern associated with thinking about yourself. Not identical to thinking about a stranger, but meaningfully less self-like than you'd expect, given that it's supposedly you. If that's even partly true, it reframes the entire saving problem: you're not failing to prioritize your own future. You're failing to fully recognize that the future person benefiting from today's sacrifice and the present person making the sacrifice are the same entity — and asking someone to give something up for a person who doesn't feel fully like themselves is a much harder ask than the math alone would suggest.

Why would a mind be built this way? Because for almost all of human history, the future was radically less certain than it is for most people reading this now — resources not used today might never get the chance to be used at all, consumed by circumstance, taken by someone else, lost to an unpredictable world. A mind that heavily favored the present wasn't being short-sighted in that environment. It was correctly pricing in a level of future uncertainty that made "now" a genuinely safer bet than "later," most of the time. The mismatch, as with the other patterns in this book, is that the modern financial world offers a level of future certainty — compounding, retirement systems, long-horizon planning — that this ancient discounting instinct was never calibrated for, and it still runs the old math regardless.

There's a version of present bias that shows up specifically around health-adjacent spending, where the future cost isn't just financial but physical, and the discounting compounds across both dimensions at once. Skipping a preventive expense — a checkup, an ergonomic fix, a piece of safety equipment — saves present-you a small, felt cost today, while quietly discounting a future cost that is often larger in both dollars and consequence, and further away, which makes it doubly easy to underweight. The same instinct that discounts a retirement contribution discounts a knee that will need surgery in fifteen years because a smaller intervention wasn't made now, and the two are, structurally, the identical mechanism, just wearing different clothes.

This shows up as more than just under-saving. It's the reason a future deadline feels manageable right up until it doesn't. The work gets pushed toward present-you's comfort, again and again, because future-you doesn't feel urgent or real enough. Future-you is the one who'll have to deal with the consequence — but that doesn't outweigh today's smaller, felt discomfort of starting now. It's the reason a health habit with a payoff decades out is so much harder to sustain than one with an immediate felt benefit, even when the long-term stakes are far higher. Anywhere a present cost buys a future benefit, this same discounting runs, and it runs hardest exactly when the future benefit is largest and most distant — which is, unfortunately, exactly the shape of most serious long-term saving.

There's a further layer worth naming from psychologist E. Tory Higgins's research on self-discrepancy theory, which distinguishes between the "actual self" — who you are right now — and the "ideal self" — who you'd like to become. Future-you, in the context of saving, is meant to function as a version of the ideal self: secure, provided-for, unburdened by decisions you failed to make today. But because present bias keeps that ideal future self feeling abstract and distant rather than vivid and connected, the gap between actual and ideal never gets the emotional weight it would need to actually motivate consistent present-day sacrifice. Higgins's broader finding is that the size of the felt gap between actual and ideal self matters enormously for motivation — a gap that feels real and close drives action, while a gap that feels theoretical and far away barely registers at all. This is, in effect, the same insight as the Hershfield research on vivid future-self imagery, arrived at from a different direction: the problem was never that people don't want a secure future self. It's that the future self doesn't feel real enough, soon enough, to compete with a present want that is, by definition, already fully real.

What it costs you

The direct cost compounds in the most literal financial sense there is: money not saved today doesn't just fail to exist for future-you, it fails to exist *and* to have grown, for every year between now and whenever it would have been needed. Present bias doesn't cost you a fixed amount. It costs you a fixed amount multiplied by every year of compounding that amount would otherwise have had — which means the earliest years of underfunding a future goal are, mathematically, the most expensive years to skip, precisely because they're the ones that would have compounded the longest.

There's a version of this cost worth naming specifically around health insurance and coverage decisions, where present bias shows up as choosing the cheapest available option today without adequately weighting the meaningfully worse position a future version of you might be in if a real health event occurs before better coverage is in place. The premium saved today is immediate and felt; the protection given up is abstract and, by definition, only matters in a future scenario that present-you would rather not spend energy imagining. This is present bias operating at its most consequential, because unlike a missed retirement contribution, which can often be partially made up later, a coverage gap that turns out to matter can produce a cost that dwarfs anything saved by the cheaper premium, arriving at exactly the moment a person is least equipped to absorb a financial shock on top of everything else going on.

The deeper cost is the one future-you eventually inherits without ever having had a vote in creating it. Present bias doesn't disappear when you get older — it simply relocates the burden onto whichever version of you happens to become "present" once the deferred decisions can't be deferred any further. The stranger you were discounting all along eventually becomes the one who is you, in the fullest, most immediate sense, and by then the decisions that would have helped were made, or not made, by someone who no longer exists to answer for them. This is the quiet cruelty of present bias: it never actually saves you from the cost. It only ever chooses who has to pay it.

The overrides

You can't out-argue present bias with statistics about future benefit — the gap isn't informational, it's a felt failure to fully register future-you as the same person making the sacrifice today.

Apply the future-receipt exercise specifically to preventive health and coverage decisions. Because present bias hits health-adjacent spending with particularly steep consequences, run the concrete-future-self exercise explicitly on any decision where skipping a present cost creates real future risk — a checkup skipped, a coverage gap accepted, a warning sign deferred. Picture the specific future version of you who inherits the consequence, not in the abstract, but in a particular room, at a particular age, dealing with a particular version of the problem that a small present action would have prevented or reduced.

Make future-you concrete, not abstract. The discounting is strongest when future-you is a vague, faceless idea. Make that person specific instead: picture an actual age, an actual scene, an actual version of your life at that point, and let that concrete image stand in for the abstract "future" your mind is currently underweighting. This isn't a sentimental exercise — research on this exact intervention has found that making the future self feel more vivid and real measurably increases people's willingness to save for it, because it closes some of the psychological distance the discounting instinct depends on.

Anchor short-distance and long-distance discounting decisions to the same standard. Because the discounting rate isn't constant across distances, notice when you're treating a one-month decision more patiently than an identical one-month gap that happens to start today rather than a year from now. Deliberately apply your calmer, more patient "distant" reasoning to present-moment choices as well, since the underlying trade-off — smaller now versus larger soon — genuinely hasn't changed, only its felt proximity has.

Automate the handoff so present-you never has to decide twice. Present bias wins its battles in individual, repeated moments of choice — should I save this or spend it, asked over and over. Remove the repeated choice entirely. Set up the transfer, the contribution, the automatic allocation once, in a calm moment, so future-you's interests are served by default rather than by a fresh act of willpower every single time. This is the same principle from the lifestyle-creep chapter, applied here: money that moves before present-you has a chance to discount it never enters the discounting calculation at all.

Name the discounting-rate mismatch explicitly, if you're planning with someone else. If a savings disagreement with a partner keeps circling without resolution, check whether it's actually a values disagreement or a difference in how vivid each of your future selves feels. Naming that difference directly — "my future self feels close and real to me, does yours?" — often does more to resolve the friction than another round of arguing about the specific number, because it locates the actual mechanism instead of treating the symptom.

Give yourself a future receipt. For a purely present-focused purchase, briefly imagine the equivalent future version of the decision — what would this same amount, redirected instead, have become by the time future-you needed it? This isn't meant to guilt you out of every present expense; present-you matters too, and this book isn't asking you to live entirely for someone who doesn't exist yet. It's meant to make the trade-off visible in both directions, instead of only in the direction present bias already favors by default.

Practice on the short-distance version first. Because present bias runs at every timescale, not just the decades-long one, you can build the muscle for it on cheaper, faster feedback loops before applying it to retirement-length decisions. Pick one recurring short-horizon choice — the meal-prep, the small extra payment, the modest weekly transfer — and deliberately choose the future-favoring option for a month. The near-term payoff arrives fast enough to actually be felt, which does more to retrain the discounting instinct than any amount of abstract reasoning about compound interest thirty years out ever will.

The rule to remember: *Future you is not a stranger — it's you, on a delay. Every dollar you protect today is a message to someone who will absolutely receive it, whether or not it feels that way right now.*

Chapter 12 — The Mental Envelopes

The quiet accounting error your brain makes with money every single day

A tax refund arrives, and it goes toward something fun — a trip, a splurge, something the same amount from a regular paycheck would never have been spent on. A twenty-dollar bill found in an old coat pocket gets spent without a second thought, in a way twenty dollars transferred from savings never would be. Casino winnings get gambled back with a looseness that the same amount, earned through a week of work, would never be treated with. In every case, the money is identical — a dollar is a dollar, fungible, interchangeable, worth exactly the same regardless of where it came from. And in every case, your mind treats it as if it weren't.

There's a version of this that operates across accounts rather than within a single budget, and it's often the most expensive version because it involves larger sums held for longer periods. Someone can hold a meaningful sum in a low-yield savings account, mentally filed as "emergency fund, don't touch," while simultaneously carrying a credit card balance at a far higher interest rate, mentally filed as "debt, dealing with it separately" — two envelopes, two different sets of rules, the same person, the same overall financial picture, and a arrangement that a single unified view of the money would immediately flag as backwards. The emergency fund isn't earning enough to justify not using part of it to pay down the more expensive debt; but "emergency fund" and "debt" are different envelopes in this person's mind, governed by different rules, and the money never gets compared to itself across the wall the envelopes have built.

Watch it happen at a smaller scale too, inside a single budget. Money set aside for "entertainment" gets spent freely, down to the last dollar, right up against the boundary of that category — while an equivalent amount sitting in a "miscellaneous" or "savings" envelope goes untouched, even in a month where the entertainment money could easily have covered the same need. The categories aren't real. They're lines your own mind drew, and yet they behave, in practice, like solid walls that money isn't allowed to cross, no matter how much sense crossing them would actually make.

This is one of the last patterns in this book, and it's worth calling out as the one that ties most of the others together, because it's less a single trigger and more a structural quirk in how your mind organizes money in the first place — one that quietly amplifies almost every other pattern already covered.

Watch it operate in a household budget across a full year and the envelopes reveal something almost comic in how inconsistent they are with each other. The same family that agonizes over a twenty-dollar overage in the "dining out" envelope will, without a second thought, spend four hundred dollars on a holiday gift exchange filed under "seasonal" — a category that somehow feels exempt from the scrutiny every other envelope receives, simply because it only comes around once a year and has always been treated as its own separate thing. Ask them to justify the discrepancy and there usually isn't one, beyond "that's just what the holidays cost" — a mental envelope with its own permissive rules, sitting right alongside the strict ones, in the same household, governing the exact same fungible dollars.

What's actually happening

The mechanism is called mental accounting, and the researcher most responsible for naming and mapping it is Richard Thaler, whose broader work on the gap between how people actually handle money and how a purely rational accounting would handle it runs through several of the patterns in this book. The core finding here: rather than treating all money as one interchangeable pool, your mind sorts it into separate mental envelopes — the grocery envelope, the fun-money envelope, the found-money envelope, the bonus envelope — and money in one envelope gets treated by entirely different rules than the identical amount sitting in another, even though, on any bank statement, it's all just one number.

There's a version of mental accounting that runs at the level of an entire income source rather than a single transaction, and it's worth naming because it can distort major life decisions rather than just small purchases. Freelance or variable income often gets mentally filed as inherently less "real" or less stable than a salaried paycheck, even when, averaged across a year, it amounts to the same or more — which leads to systematically different treatment: less aggressive saving, less confidence in large purchases, a persistent low-grade sense of precariousness that the actual numbers don't fully support. The envelope here isn't about a specific dollar amount at all. It's about an entire category of income being pre-labeled as fragile, regardless of its actual track record, purely because of the label attached to how consistently it arrives rather than how much it totals.

This sorting isn't random or meaningless — in a lot of ways, it's a genuinely useful shortcut, a way of imposing structure on money that would otherwise be an undifferentiated blur. The trouble comes from the specific rules different envelopes get assigned, because the rules are rarely consistent with the money's actual, fungible nature. Money labeled "found" — a refund, a windfall, a gift — gets treated as lower-stakes, more disposable, more appropriate for spending loosely, purely because of the label attached to how it arrived, not because of anything about what it's actually worth or what it could otherwise do. Money labeled "earned through effort" gets treated more cautiously. Money sitting in a "savings" envelope feels protected, almost untouchable, even while money in a "checking" envelope, doing functionally the same job, gets spent freely — sometimes while the "protected" savings money is simultaneously earning less interest than a debt elsewhere is costing, an arrangement that makes no rational sense once you see both envelopes as what they actually are: one pool, arbitrarily divided.

There's a specific version worth naming around tax refunds in particular, because they sit at the exact intersection of several of this chapter's dynamics at once: a tax refund is, structurally, just a return of your own money that was withheld throughout the year — not a bonus, not a gift, not found money in any real sense, since it was yours all along and the government simply held it interest-free. And yet it is one of the most reliably "found-money-labeled" categories of income there is, spent looser than an equivalent paycheck with striking consistency. The label wins over the facts almost every time: knowing, intellectually, that a refund isn't really a windfall does little to stop it from being treated like one, which is as clean a demonstration as exists of how much more power the mental envelope's label carries than the underlying financial reality it's supposedly just organizing.

There's a version of mental accounting worth naming that shows up specifically around gift-giving during holidays, where an entire season's spending gets mentally carved out into its own envelope, exempt from the scrutiny the rest of the year's budget receives. This isn't unique to any one household; it's close to a cultural default — "holiday spending" is treated, almost universally, as a special category with its own permissive rules, justified by tradition and occasion rather than by any actual accounting logic. The cost of this particular envelope is easy to underestimate precisely because it recurs every single year with the same social permission slip attached, meaning the same mental accounting exemption gets re-applied annually, compounding across a lifetime into a genuinely large total that never once got evaluated against the rest of the household's actual priorities.

Here's where this pattern quietly compounds nearly every other one in this book. The windfall that triggers a dopamine-driven spending spree is doing so partly because it landed in the "found money" envelope, which your mind has already pre-approved for looser spending. The raise that vanishes into lifestyle creep is, in part, a mental accounting failure — the new income gets filed into the "available to spend" envelope by default, rather than being deliberately routed into a "protected" envelope before the creep can claim it. Even the endowment effect interacts with this: money already assigned to a specific mental envelope, like a long-held investment account, can feel harder to reallocate than the same amount would if it were still sitting, unlabeled, in a general pool. The envelopes aren't a separate problem from everything else in this book. They're the accounting system all the other patterns are quietly running on top of.

There's a compounding piece worth naming from psychologist Jennifer Crocker and Connie Wolfe's research on contingencies of self-worth — the finding that people's sense of their own value gets tied, often unconsciously, to specific domains of performance, and money is one of the domains where this attaches most easily. When self-worth is contingent on being seen as financially responsible, mental accounting can become a tool for managing that self-image rather than a tool for managing money: keeping the "savings" envelope untouched isn't really about the interest math anymore, it's about being able to tell yourself, and anyone who asks, that you're someone who saves — even while carrying debt that makes the arrangement mathematically indefensible. The envelope becomes less an accounting device and more a piece of evidence in an ongoing, private case for a particular self-image, which is part of why pointing out the mathematical inconsistency so rarely changes anyone's behavior on its own. The envelope was never really doing math. It was doing identity maintenance, and identity maintenance has its own stubborn logic that a spreadsheet can't touch.

What it costs you

The direct cost shows up any time money in a low-priority envelope is spent freely while money in a high-priority envelope, doing a worse job, is preserved out of habit rather than logic — carrying high-interest debt while maintaining a low-interest savings cushion is the clearest version of this, a arrangement that only makes sense if you're treating the two pools as genuinely separate rather than as the single, interchangeable pool they actually are.

There's a version of this cost worth naming around business finances specifically, where mental accounting can distort decisions at a much larger scale than any household budget. A small business owner who treats revenue from a new product line as a separate envelope from the core business's cash flow may make wildly different, and wildly inconsistent, decisions about risk, reinvestment, and reserves across the two pools, even though both pools ultimately answer to the same balance sheet and the same underlying business. Money "earned" in the exciting new venture gets reinvested aggressively, treated with the same looseness as found money; money in the "core business" envelope gets guarded cautiously — and the business as a whole ends up with a risk profile that reflects the arbitrary accounting split rather than any deliberate, unified strategy anyone actually chose.

The deeper cost is a subtler kind of leak: every dollar's fate gets decided partly by which envelope it happened to land in, rather than by where it would actually do the most good — which means a meaningful portion of your total financial life is being governed not by your priorities, but by the arbitrary circumstances of how each dollar arrived. A raise and a refund of the same size can produce wildly different outcomes purely because of the label attached on arrival, even though, once they're both sitting in your account, they are, in every way that matters, the exact same money.

The overrides

You can't eliminate mental accounting altogether — some structure is genuinely useful, and a mind with zero categorical sorting of money would likely make worse decisions, not better ones. The goal isn't to stop using envelopes. It's to make sure the envelopes are serving your actual priorities instead of arbitrary labels.

Give tax refunds and similarly-labeled income a mandatory pause before spending. Because refunds and similar "found" income are spent looser almost regardless of what people intellectually know about their source, apply a structural rule rather than relying on that knowledge alone: any income landing in the found-money category sits untouched for a fixed period — thirty days is reasonable — before any discretionary spending decision gets made on it. The delay does the work the intellectual reframe alone usually can't, because it separates the decision from the moment the label's pull is strongest.

Practice one-pool thinking before any windfall decision. The moment money arrives with a "found" or "bonus" label attached, deliberately strip the label before deciding what to do with it. Ask: if this exact amount had shown up as part of a regular paycheck instead, what would I do with it? Usually the honest answer is more conservative than what the found-money framing was about to produce, and that gap is the mental accounting bias, made visible enough to correct.

Apply one-pool thinking to variable and freelance income specifically. If your income arrives irregularly, deliberately smooth out how you treat it mentally by averaging it over a full year rather than reacting to each individual payment's size and timing as its own separate event. This directly counters the tendency to pre-label variable income as inherently less stable than it may actually be once measured honestly across a longer window.

Label envelopes by goal, not by source. Instead of organizing money by where it came from — paycheck, refund, gift, bonus — organize it by what it's for: the emergency envelope, the near-term goal envelope, the long-term envelope, the genuinely-discretionary envelope. This keeps the useful structure of mental accounting intact while removing the arbitrary part, because now the rules attached to each envelope are based on its actual purpose rather than on the accident of how the money arrived.

Do a cross-account fungibility sweep, not just a within-budget one. Once, deliberately, lay out every account you hold — savings, checking, debt balances, investment accounts — on one page, as if they were a single pool rather than separate envelopes, and look at the interest rates and purposes side by side. This surfaces the expensive cross-account version of mental accounting that a single-budget review misses entirely, because the mismatch this catches — a low-yield "untouchable" account sitting next to high-interest debt — is usually invisible until the accounts are actually placed next to each other on the same page.

Give holiday and gift spending an actual budget line instead of an exemption. Rather than treating seasonal spending as an automatically-exempt category, set a specific number for it in advance, as part of the same planning process every other category goes through. This doesn't require spending less out of guilt — it requires the number to be chosen deliberately, on purpose, rather than inherited by default from the cultural permission slip attached to the season.

Run the fungibility test on any envelope that feels untouchable. For money that feels protected purely by habit — a savings account you won't touch even while carrying debt that costs more than the savings earns — ask directly: if I treated this as one interchangeable pool instead of two separate ones, what would the correct move actually be? Very often the answer is uncomfortable precisely because the envelope structure has been protecting an arrangement that wouldn't survive being looked at as a single pool of money, which is, in fact, all it ever was.

For business finances, unify the view before setting risk rules separately. If you run a business with more than one revenue stream, look at the combined balance sheet before deciding, deliberately and explicitly, how much risk each stream should be allowed to carry — rather than letting each stream inherit its own risk tolerance purely from the accounting convenience of having been tracked separately. The separation can stay for bookkeeping purposes; the risk decisions should be made with the full picture in view.

The rule to remember: *A dollar doesn't know where it came from, and it shouldn't decide where it goes based on that either. Sort your money by what it's for, not by how it arrived.*

Before You Go

You've now met all eleven of them: the loop that mistakes wanting for having, the creep that swallows every raise, the audience that was never watching, the anchor that isn't yours, the scarcity tunnel that outlasts the shortage, the reflex that panics at exactly the wrong moment, the envelope you can't bring yourself to open, the sunk cost that has no vote in what happens next, the endowment that inflates what's already yours, the stranger who turns out to be you on a delay, and the mental envelopes sorting your money by accident instead of by purpose.

Read back over that list and one thing should be obvious: none of it was ever about being bad with money. Every single pattern in this book is a normal, predictable, well-documented feature of a mind that was built for a world very different from the one your money actually lives in now. Your money behavior isn't a character flaw. It's a wiring feature — inherited, functional in its original context, and simply mismatched to a modern financial world of one-tap purchases, decades-long compounding, and abstractions no ancestor of yours ever had to price.

It's worth being honest, too, about what this book cannot do, because overpromising here would undercut the very method it's asking you to trust. Building a structural override doesn't mean the underlying instinct goes quiet forever, never to be felt again. The dopamine loop will still spike when a countdown timer appears. The status instinct will still flicker when a friend shows up with something new. What changes isn't the presence of the feeling — it's what happens in the gap between the feeling and the decision. A person with a working override still feels the pull. They just no longer let the pull make the call alone, because something structural got there first. That's a smaller promise than "you'll stop wanting things," and it's also a far more honest and durable one, because it doesn't depend on ever fully outgrowing wiring that isn't going anywhere.

That reframe is not a way of excusing anything. It's the thing that finally makes change possible, because you cannot fix a character flaw with information — people have been trying that for as long as personal finance books have existed, and it mostly doesn't work, which is exactly why this book didn't try it. But you *can* build a specific override for a specific, identifiable mechanism, the way you've now done eleven times over. That's a fundamentally different kind of work than trying to become a different, more disciplined person. It's closer to engineering than to willpower — and engineering, unlike willpower, doesn't get tired, doesn't require you to feel motivated on a given day, and doesn't quietly erode over time the way sheer discipline reliably does.

If you're looking for a place to start and nothing in particular jumped out, here's a rough diagnostic worth trying: think back to the last time money caused you real stress, embarrassment, or regret — not a minor annoyance, but a moment that actually stuck with you. Which chapter's opening scene comes closest to describing what happened? That's very often the pattern doing the most damage in your specific life, even if it isn't the one that felt most relatable on a first read-through. The patterns that cost the most aren't always the ones that are easiest to recognize in yourself; sometimes the most expensive one is also the one you've gotten best at explaining away.

You don't need to run all eleven overrides simultaneously starting tomorrow. Go back to whichever one or two chapters felt most like they were describing you specifically — most people find it's one or two, not all eleven — and start there. Build that override into your life as a structure, not a New Year's resolution. Once it's running quietly in the background, requiring no daily willpower to maintain, move to the next one.

If you take nothing else from these eleven chapters, take this: the mechanism that's been costing you the most is very likely not the one that feels the most dramatic. The panic-sell makes headlines, in your own life if nowhere else — it's the story you tell about the one bad financial decision you remember clearly. But for most people, reading honestly, the real damage runs quieter than that: a raise that vanished without a single bad decision anywhere in the chain, an envelope left unopened for a season too long, a jacket bought for a witness who was never in the room. The quiet patterns are the expensive ones precisely because they never trigger the alarm a dramatic mistake does. Nothing about them ever felt like a crisis worth fixing. That's exactly why they got to run, uninterrupted, for as long as they have.

The argument in your head that opened this book — the fast, certain voice and the slower, quieter one that shows up a day too late — doesn't go away once you understand it. It's not supposed to. The goal was never to silence the fast voice; it's not going anywhere, and a life with none of it would be a strange, joyless one anyway. The goal was only ever to make sure the slower voice gets into the room *before* the decision, instead of arriving afterward to do the math on what already happened. That's the whole system, in one sentence: not winning the argument, but making sure both sides show up on time.

Notes & Further Reading

The mechanisms described in this book draw on real, established research in psychology and behavioral economics. This book is a work of synthesis and application, not original research — every named finding below belongs to the researchers credited, and readers interested in going deeper should start with their original work.

Chapter 1 — The Machine You Didn't Install. The concept of self-efficacy — learned beliefs about what one is and isn't capable of controlling, shaped by direct experience and observed example — comes from psychologist Albert Bandura's research program on social cognitive theory. The distinction between the content of a thought and one's relationship to it draws on psychologist Steven Hayes's work developing acceptance and commitment therapy.

Chapter 2 — The Dopamine Loop. The distinction between the "wanting" and "liking" systems in the brain's reward circuitry, and the finding that dopamine tracks reward *prediction* more than reward receipt, comes from decades of work in behavioral neuroscience, notably associated with researcher Kent Berridge and collaborators on the neuroscience of incentive salience. The "mere exposure effect" — increased favorability toward a stimulus through repeated exposure alone — was documented by psychologist Robert Zajonc.

Chapter 3 — The Creep. Hedonic adaptation, sometimes called the "hedonic treadmill," is a well-established finding in the psychology of well-being, describing how quickly people adjust to positive changes in circumstance and return to a relatively stable baseline of satisfaction. Adaptation-level theory, describing how judgments of "normal" recalibrate continuously against recent experience, draws on the broader tradition of comparison research associated with Leon Festinger and later adaptation researchers.

Chapter 4 — The Audience That Isn't There. Social comparison theory was formalized by psychologist Leon Festinger in the 1950s. The related concept of conspicuous consumption — spending oriented toward display rather than use — was introduced by economist Thorstein Veblen in his 1899 work analyzing consumption and social status. The "front stage" and "backstage" self framework comes from sociologist Erving Goffman's work on the presentation of self in everyday life.

Chapter 5 — The Anchor. Anchoring, including the classic wheel-of-fortune experiment described in this chapter, comes from the research of psychologists Daniel Kahneman and Amos Tversky, whose decades of collaborative work on judgment under uncertainty reshaped the field of behavioral economics and contributed to Kahneman's 2002 Nobel Memorial Prize in Economic Sciences. The dual-process distinction between fast, automatic thinking and slower, deliberate thinking is further developed in Kahneman's later work.

Chapter 6 — The Scarcity Brain. The cognitive-bandwidth model of scarcity, including the concept of "tunneling," comes from the research of economist Sendhil Mullainathan and psychologist Eldar Shafir, published in their work examining how scarcity shapes decision-making across contexts including poverty, time pressure, and loneliness. The distinction between problem-focused and emotion-focused coping comes from psychologist Richard Lazarus's research on stress and appraisal.

Chapter 7 — The Worst-Time Reflex. Loss aversion — the finding that losses are felt more intensely than equivalent gains — is a central pillar of prospect theory, developed by Daniel Kahneman and Amos Tversky and first published in their landmark 1979 paper. The discussion of cognitive dissonance draws on Leon Festinger's separate, foundational research on the discomfort produced by conflicting beliefs and actions.

Chapter 8 — The Unopened Envelope. The framing of financial avoidance as anxiety management, rather than simple negligence, draws on broader research in the psychology of avoidance coping and information-seeking behavior under threat of negative news. The discussion of identity-protective information processing draws on political scientist Dan Kahan's research on identity-protective cognition.

Chapter 9 — The Sunk-Cost Trap. The sunk-cost fallacy and its treatment within behavioral economics is closely associated with the work of economist Richard Thaler, whose research on the gap between rational-actor models and actual human financial behavior contributed to his 2017 Nobel Memorial Prize in Economic Sciences. The discussion of consistency pressure around public commitments draws on the broader social-psychology literature on commitment and consistency associated with researchers including Barry Schwartz. The discussion of self-verification draws on psychologist William Swann's research on the motivation to have one's existing self-concept confirmed.

Chapter 10 — The Endowment Trap. The endowment effect, including mug-based valuation experiments of the kind described in this chapter, was documented in research by Richard Thaler and further explored in collaborative work with Daniel Kahneman and Jack Knetsch. The status quo bias — a documented preference for current arrangements independent of their merits — was identified by economists William Samuelson and Richard Zeckhauser.

Chapter 11 — The Stranger That Is Future You. Present bias and temporal discounting are established findings in behavioral economics; research on neural responses to future-self versus present-self reasoning has been explored by researchers including Hal Hershfield, whose work examines interventions that increase saving by making the future self feel more psychologically vivid and connected to the present one. Self-discrepancy theory, describing the motivational gap between one's actual and ideal self, comes from psychologist E. Tory Higgins.

Chapter 12 — The Mental Envelopes. Mental accounting — the tendency to treat money differently depending on its mental category rather than its fungible, interchangeable nature — was named and extensively documented by Richard Thaler across multiple papers examining real-world financial decision-making. The discussion of contingencies of self-worth draws on research by psychologists Jennifer Crocker and Connie Wolfe.

Any errors of interpretation or application in how these findings are described are the author's alone. This book simplifies genuinely complex research for a general audience; readers who want the full nuance should go to the original sources.

About

The Money Instinct comes from the studio behind the Money Instinct project — a psychology-of-money brand built on one premise: the gap between knowing what to do with money and actually doing it is rarely about information. It's about the wiring underneath the decision. This book, and the material that follows it, is an ongoing exploration of that gap and what actually closes it — not through more advice about what to do with your money, but through a clearer view of the machine making the decision in the first place, and the specific, structural moves that let its slower, wiser voice into the room on time.

Before You Close This Book

You've read all eleven now, and one or two of them almost certainly felt uncomfortably specific. That discomfort is useful information, not a verdict on your character — it's simply pointing you toward the pattern doing the most quiet damage in your particular life right now. If even one of these eleven patterns felt like it was describing you specifically, there's a next step. A short assessment — "What's Your Money Instinct?" — maps which of these patterns is likely running strongest in your specific life, so you're not guessing which override to build first, and so the next thing you build is the one actually worth building right now, rather than whichever chapter happened to be freshest in your mind when you closed the book.

The full system, worked examples, and a companion set of exercises live at the Money Instinct's home online. Whatever you build first — a twenty-four-hour rule, a standing money date, a single automated transfer that runs before you ever see the money — build it small enough to actually survive an ordinary, imperfect week, because a small override still running six months from now will always outperform an ambitious one abandoned by February.

The machine got you this far. Now you know how to work with it instead of against it — one specific override, built once, running quietly in the background of an ordinary week, for as long as you need it to.

Also in the Series

Every book in The Money Instinct library stands on its own — read them in any order. If this one was useful, the library continues:

The Secrecy Instinct

The Underearning Instinct

The Shame Instinct

The Panic Instinct

The Merge Instinct

The Ceiling Instinct

The Windfall Instinct

The Control Instinct

The Legacy Instinct

The Comparison Instinct

The Enabling Instinct

The Austerity Instinct

The Paralysis Instinct

The Retirement Instinct

The Divorce Instinct

The Enough Instinct

The Overconfidence Instinct

The Vigilance Instinct

The Generosity Instinct

www.ingramcontent.com/pod-product-compliance
Lightning Source LLC
LaVergne TN
LVHW010718061126
851857LV00014B/1238